Charles Alexander McMurry

A Course of Study for the Eight Grades of the Common School

Including a Hand Book of Practical Suggestions to Teachers

Charles Alexander McMurry

A Course of Study for the Eight Grades of the Common School Including a Hand Book of Practical Suggestions to Teachers

ISBN/EAN: 9783337778248

Printed in Europe, USA, Canada, Australia, Japan

Cover: Foto ©Paul-Georg Meister /pixelio.de

More available books at **www.hansebooks.com**

A Course of Study

FOR THE

Eight Grades

OF THE

Common School

INCLUDING A

Hand Book of Practical Suggestions to Teachers

BY

Charles A. McMurry, Ph.D.

BLOOMINGTON, ILL.
PUBLIC-SCHOOL PUBLISHING COMPANY
1895

TABLE OF CONTENTS.

	Page.
First Year,	7
Second Year,	22
Third Grade,	39
Fourth Grade,	54
Fifth Grade,	69
Sixth Grade,	84
Seventh Grade,	99
Eighth Grade,	127
Preparatory Class,	141
Hand Book,	143

THIS COURSE OF STUDY

IS DEDICATED TO

The Teachers of the Common Schools.

In making out their Courses of Study for local use, superintendents
and teachers are at liberty to make such use of the materials and suggestions of this book as they may
desire, giving credit for the same.
The author will be gratified to
receive such courses of
study for compar-
ison.

Preface.

This course of study has been worked out in the training department of a Normal School, where it may, perhaps, suit the conditions, but in any other school it would need to be more or less modified. Some of the peculiar conditions of such a school may be stated thus:

1. A very large teaching force of from one hundred to a hundred and twenty pupil-teachers is at hand. A teacher has usually but a single class in one study, one period (45 minutes, sometimes only 22 minutes) daily.

2. Out of six regular recitation periods daily the children usually recite during five periods and have but one study period in school. The method of teaching is therefore largely oral and the recitation period is a learning period. This oral teaching calls for greater skill and mastery, if it is to be effective.

3. There is usually but one class in the room at a time, and that a small one (from ten to twenty pupils).

4. In intermediate and grammar grades only arithmetic and reading are recited daily. In other words there are three pairs of alternating studies. Literature or history alternates with natural science; geography alternates with language lessons; writing alternates with drawing. Each of these studies is, therefore, only a half study, coming only every other day. The daily program for any class may appear, therefore, as follows:

Opening exercises and spelling. 25 minutes.

1. Period. Arithmetic, daily, 45 minutes.
2. Period. History or Literature—Natural Science. 45 minutes.

Recess.

3. Period. Reading, daily, 45 minutes.
4. Period. Writing —Drawing. 45 minutes.

Noon.

5. Period.   Geography—Language Lessons, 45 minutes.
6. Period.   Study period, 45 minutes.

5. A room teacher is responsible for each room, who takes charge of the room at recesses and during the study period and teaches some of the classes. The room teacher, with the aid of the critic teacher, seeks to give unity and consistency to the work of so many different instructors.

In the following course of study there is an effort to incorporate such improvements as the progress of education is demanding. The doctrine of *concentration* has influenced the choice and arrangement of materials not a little. Not that this course is a full or even satisfactory working out of that doctrine, but only a positive beginning along this line. Concentration is a very large and comprehensive problem and can be worked out only gradually. Not much effort is made in this course to correlate arithmetic with the other studies, and in writing, drawing, and music not very much is yet accomplished, but in history and literature, reading, geography, natural science, and language, there seems to be already a natural and legitimate field for correlating studies.

For a fuller discussion of material and method in each study, practicing teachers are constantly referred to the Special Methods in Reading, Literature and History, Geography, and Natural Science, besides other books of method. A second series of books, which furnishes the full treatment of topics, is partly worked out for the grades. For these, consult the price-list at the end of this book.

Several teachers have assisted in this work, whose names are given in the body of the book.

Normal, Ill., Sept. 7, 1895.

First Year.

Literature.

First Term. Fall.

1. The Old Woman and Her Pig.
2. Little Red Riding Hood.
3. The Anxious Leaf. (Beecher.)
4. The Three Bears.
5. The Lion and the Mouse. (Æsop.)
6. The Little Match Girl. (Andersen.)

Second Term. Winter.

7. The Fir Tree. (Andersen.)
8. The Four Musicians. (Grimm.)
9. The Discontented Pine Tree.
10. Cinderella.
11. The Coal of Fire, the Bean, and the Straw. (Grimm.)

Third Term. Spring.

12. The Bird with No Name. (Grimm.)
13. The Proud Apple Branch. (Andersen.)
14. The Ugly Duckling. (Andersen.)
15. The Pea Blossom. (Andersen.)

(a) These stories, as a whole, are simple, lively, and imaginative, and call out a strong, spontaneous activity of the children.

(b) They deal with social relations and personal conduct, and also with interesting forms of plant and animal life.

(c) The first story appears very fantastic and unreal to many people, but experience shows that it has peculiar attractiveness and interest to children. Its simple repetitions make it easy to grasp and reproduce.

Several of the selections, while possessing the merits already mentioned, are suited to certain seasons and are used at those times, thus, the time of teaching "The Anxious Leaf" is determined by that of the falling of the leaves in the autumn. "The Little Match Girl" and "The Fir Tree" are both Christmas stories: the one is taught immediately before, and the other soon after the holidays. All the stories taught in the spring are specially adapted to that season of the year.

Science Topics.
Fall Term.

(1) Preparation of large buds of trees, *e. g.* hickory, buckeye, cottonwood, balm of Gilead, and walnut, for winter rest, associated with gathering of autumn leaves.

(2) Life history of dog and cow.

(3) Sheep, by comparison with cow.

(4) Fox squirrel—its home life.

(5) Rabbit and mouse by comparison with squirrel.

Winter Term.

(1) Winter study of Austrian Pine as a type of evergreen trees:

  (2) Scotch Pine.
      Hemlock.   { By comparison with
      Norway Spruce.   }   Austrian Pine.

(3) Horse.

(4) Donkey by comparison with horse.

(5) Chicken—type of birds.

(6) English sparrow and chickadee by comparison with chicken.

(7) Cat.

Spring Term.

(1) Plant sweet peas, Lima beans, and corn. Watch development.

(2) Spring study of evergreen trees studied in the winter.

(3) Robin and red-headed woodpecker.
(4) Buds and blossoms of apple, cherry, and plum.
(5) Duck—type of water bird.
(6) Goose—by comparison with the duck.
Children draw the objects studied.

Books for reference:—For study of trees, see Mrs. Dyson's "Stories of the Trees;" Gordon's "Pinetum;" Apgar's "Trees of Northern U. S.;" Gray's "Structural Botany;" Gray's "Physiological Botany."

For study of Quadrupeds see Dr. Lockwood's "Animal Memoirs," Part I.

For study of Gnawers, see:
    (1) Standard Natural History, pp. 68-133.
    (2) Seaside and Wayside IV.
    (3) Johonnot's "Feathers and Fur."
    (4) Johonnot's "Claws and Hoofs."
    (5) Wood's "Homes Without Hands."
    (6) Naturalist's Rambles About Home.
    (7) Mammals of North America (Baird).
    (8) Squirrels—Intelligence, May 1, 1894.

For study of Birds see Dr. Lockwood's "Animal Memoirs," Part II, and books by John Burroughs, Olive Thorne Miller, Leander Keyser, and Bradford Torrey.

Remarks on Nature Study.
First Term. Fall.

[The figures used in the general remarks refer to the course in Literature.]

1. (*a*) The Shepherd Dog.
   (*b*) Cow.
   (*c*) Sheep (by comparison with the cow).

The principal objects studied are *types*, and while the children do not recognize them as such in this grade, they do get a very vivid perception of the characteristic typical notions which these animals illustrate, *e.g.*, the dog is the type of *digitigrade carnivora*. The children in its study are surprised and pleased to find that it walks upon its toes. As this is the first animal studied, all comparisons are made with themselves. They like to try walking as a dog does. Its manner of eating also interests them. They see that its large tearing teeth are well adapted to devouring the kind of food it likes to eat. They do not need such teeth, for they have knife and fork; and besides, their food is cooked so that it is easily divided.

In the study of the cow, one of the most interesting points noted by them is its manner of walking on its pairs of toe-nails, or hoofs.

The teacher may well keep these type forms, based really upon scientific classification, clearly in mind, not for the purpose of imposing them upon the children too early, but to point out to him the centers of observation for children. In later years, of course, these type studies will lead up to scientific system.

The dog and the cow are two central characters in the story of "The Old Woman and Her Pig."

Another reason for choosing the dog is because every child in the class is familiar with and interested in it. For this first study at least, while the children are timid and inclined to feel school restraints as burdensome, it is important to study an animal about which all have something to say, which they will express without realizing that the school is so totally different from the home.

The shepherd dog is chosen because it is the one most commonly used in driving animals. The diversity in the appearance and character of dogs is so great that to study *the dog* would be impracticable, for while one child is thinking of a Newfoundland another might call to mind the poodle. The species familiar to the greatest number may well be chosen.

The cow is as familiar as the dog to all country children, and the city children should become acquainted with a friend to which they owe so much. No child after being in school a year should have such a vague notion of a cow as to describe it as "no bigger than my thumb nail." In many cases, by a little trouble, the city children may be taken to the suburbs to see a cow. It would be worth much to them; but if this be impossible, by the aid of good pictures and comparisons with animals familiar to them, a definite idea may be arrived at which will enable them to recognize immediately a cow which they may see later.

Usually it would seem best to study no object which cannot be presented to the class. Is not the cow an exception to the rule on account of our dependence upon it for so much of our food, clothing, etc.?

For reasons similar to those given above, the sheep is studied by all children, but let the teacher *be sure* that it is *impossible* to see the *object* before studying it otherwise.

2. We should hardly recommend the study of the wolf in connection with the story of "Little Red Riding Hood." In the first place, few of the children have seen a wolf or will be able to see one during the study. Secondly, those who do see it know little of its habits in a wild state, and it is the home life of an animal that is particularly interesting to children; thirdly, children are not dependent upon the wolf for either the luxuries or necessaries of life.

3. Preparation of familiar trees with large buds, as hickory, walnut, buckeye, and various poplars, for winter rest, this study to be associated with the gathering of autumn leaves. The connection between the Anxious Leaf and nature study is here a very close one. The leaves stay on the trees as long as needed by the buds. When the coverings of the latter are complete so that they are no longer dependent on the leaf stalks for protection, the gaily colored leaves take their well-earned holiday.

4. For reasons under (2) it seems hardly advisable to teach the bear unless the children are familiar with its habits.

5. The story of "The Lion and the Mouse" suggests among animals the *gnawers*—the mice—but in treating this group of animals with children the fox squirrel is a better type than the mouse. It is evident, therefore, that while the stories suggest the *class* of animals, the scientific type suggests the better animal for treatment than the stories. The selection of the squirrel as a type study for children depends therefore upon both literature and science. Concentration of studies does not bind us down to any slavish control of one study by another, but it leaves us free to select the best topics that literature and science, either separately or in combination, can suggest.

The nut-bearing-trees previously studied, as indicated under (3) furnish an interesting introduction to and connection with the study of the squirrels, which, about this time, are laying in their winter stores.

The rabbit is familiar to most children. By comparison with the squirrel the study deepens in interest. The season is also favorable, as the wild rabbits are abundant in the country, and their tracks in the early snows are a curious study.

The rabbit was also a friend to "The Fir Tree," about which the children learn early in the winter term.

The mouse (by comparison with the squirrel). The children are probably more familiar with the mouse than with squirrels, and enough of its habits have been brought out in a fanciful way in the story of "The Lion and the Mouse" to make this common, despised object a welcome subject of study.

Second Term. Winter.

7. and 9. A winter study of the most common evergreen of the locality, providing it be a good type of this class of

trees; this study in connection with the stories of The Fir Tree and The Unhappy Pine Tree. (a) *The Austrian Pine.*— Its foliage; two kinds of buds, leaving the children to find out for themselves in the spring what each contains; the fully grown cone, with its tightly closed doors, which a warm atmosphere causes to open; the one-year cones, whose work is only half done; position of cones on the branches; color and character of the bark; general outline of the tree. (b) the Scotch pine, (c) the Norway spruce, and the (d) Hemlock, by comparison with Austrian pine, providing these trees be common in the locality where studied.

8. The story of "The Four Musicians" suggests the study of the donkey. But first we shall study *the horse*, a cousin of the donkey, it being a better type of solid-hoofed animals. (b) The donkey (compared with the horse). (c) *The cat*, whose characteristic habits have been brought out in the story. (d) *The chicken*, another of the musicians and a good type of birds. (e) English sparrow, and (f) Chickadee, by comparison with chicken.

Any other birds common during the winter time in the locality where studied would do as well as the two mentioned above.

Third Term. Spring.

11 and 15. Plant Lima beans, sweet peas, and corn. We have heard about the bean that burst from laughing in the story of "The Bean, the Coal of Fire, and the Straw," and shall find that beans burst when working in sober earnest. The sweet peas are near relatives, and we shall need a vine and some flowers when teaching the story of "The Pea Blossom." The corn is planted that its contrast in growth from the seed, when compared with the bean and the pea, may be noted. (The gradual development of these plants from seed to flower and fruit is carefully noticed by the children.)

7 and 9. Spring study of the evergreen trees whose

winter study we have noted previously—the development of the clustered buds of the Austrian pine into staminate flowers and new growth, and of the long pointed buds into new growth and cones; the office of the sap; uses of the root, trunk, branches, and leaves; seeds sown and manner of growth studied.

12. (*a*) The robin, our best known summer bird, took part in the contest for kingship in the story of "The Bird With No Name," so also did (*b*) the red-headed wood-pecker, one of our most showy birds. For study, any other birds would do as well. These are most familiar to the children in the locality in which this course is followed. The wren, owl, and eagle are more prominent in the story, but the wren is a small bird, quite inconspicuous in color, and very frequently no child in the class knows it. Were it familiar to the children it would be desirable to study it. The owl may better be studied in the winter when material is scarce, and the eagle is not well known with us.

13. (*a*) *Apple Blossoms* connected with the story of The Proud Apple Branch. The buds are studied from the beginning of term, or at least these observations are begun before any change has taken place in the bud, and all decided changes are carefully noted by the pupils until the fruit is well formed or ripened. (*b*) Plum, and (*c*) Cherry, watched as above and compared with the apple.

14. (*a*) *The Duck* (type of water birds), studied in connection with the story of The Ugly Duckling. (*b*) *The Goose*, by comparison with the duck.

Reading.

Work for Fall Term—Cyr's Primer, pp. 1-25. "Rhymes From Verse and Prose."

Sounds of Letters—Short sounds of a, e, i, o, u; b, hard c, d, f, hard g, h, k, l, m, n, p, r, s, t, v, w, ch, ow, oy, and sonant th. No markings of sounds.

Work for Winter Term—Cyr's Primer, complete. Selections from "Heart of Oak I.," "Verse and Prose," and Æsop's Fables.

Sounds of Letters—Long sounds of a, e, i, o, u, with marking of both short and long sounds, cedilla c, soft g, nonsonant th, s when sounded like z, ou, oi, sh.

Work for Spring Term—Hodskins' Little People's Reader, pp. 1-51, and selections from "Nature Stories for Young Readers," and "Animal Life," also poems connected with their other work.

For method, see McMurry's Special Method in Reading.

First Term. Fall.

(a) The stories which the children have learned and reproduced in first grade, together with the science topics, have often been made the basis of board script exercises in learning to read. The advantage of using these thought materials in the first reading exercises is that both the words and the thoughts are familiar and interesting to the children and they enjoy learning to read stories which have attracted their interest. This is the opposite of the formal drill on charts and in primers. The subject matter in these exercises is derived from topics treated in Literature and Science.

(b) Reading, from a book, or printed page, of poems, rhymes, and songs previously learned by the children at home or in school.

1. Bow, wow, wow, whose dog art thou; Hark! hark! hark! the dogs do bark; Pretty Cow, Jane Taylor; The Cow, Robert Louis Stevenson; Little Boy Blue; Little Bopeep; Mary's Lamb; all from Verse and Prose for Beginners.

3. "I am the wind and I come very fast."

5. By Baby Bunting, and R was a rabbit; Five Little Mice; Hickory, dickory dock, and Some little mice sat in the barn to spin, from Verse and Prose.

6. The First Christmas, Emilie Poulsson; Snowflakes—"Tap, tap, tap, what a tiny call," etc.; The Snow—"Little white feathers," etc.; "Heart of Oak I." contains of these rhymes.

During this term and the following terms, beginning about the fifth or sixth week of school, the children spend a few minutes each day learning the sounds of letters, these sounds being derived by them from some of the words with which they have become familiar. Through their knowledge of these sounds they are enabled to make out words for themselves, and the second term they do considerable of the reading without previous acquaintance with the story or poem.

Second Term. Winter.

7 and 9. The moon and stars smiled down upon the little fir tree of our story, in its forest home, doing all in their power to make it happy, and the snowflakes made it a beautiful white coat.

This season also suggests the following: Star light, star bright; I have a little Sister, they call hey Peep, Peep; and Twinkle, Twinkle Little Star; from Verse and Prose. Lady Moon, Lord Houghton; I see the Moon; and O, Look at the Moon, from Heart of Oak I.; Snowflakes—"Whenever a snowflake leaves the sky"; Pine Needles, Wm. Hayne; The Snowflake's Story, in Nature Stories for Young Readers.

8. Ride a cock horse; Great A, little a; Pussy cat, pussy cat; I like little pussy: from Heart of Oak I. Hey, diddle, diddle; Ding, dong bell; Three little kittens; from Verse and Prose. Pussy sits beside the fire, Heart of Oak I.; The Little Chickadee.

Also the following of Æsop's Fables simplified:

The Old Hound; The Horse and the Groom; The Donkey and the Wolf; The Donkey and the Horse; Belling the Cat; The Cat and the Mice; The Hen and the Golden Eggs.

11. The Boy Bathing, The Bear and the Two Travelers.

Third Term. Spring.

11 and 15. A Little Brown Seed, When the Seeds Begin to Sprout: in Child's Song Book: A Dewdrop, Stevenson; The Swing, Stevenson: Runaway Brook, Mrs. Follen; from Verse and Prose. Drip, Drip, Drip, in Child's Song Book. The April Shower. Who Likes the Rain, Clara Doty Bates. Plump Little Baby Clouds, One Little Cloud. Nature Stories for Young Reader pp. 1–4, 10-12, and 28–33.

12. Nature Stories for Young Readers, pp. 12-14, 16, 17, 33-37. Animal Life, pp. 113-115; The Egg in the Nest, Who Stole the Bird's Nest, Once I Saw a Little Bird, Who Killed Cock Robin, The Bird and its Nest, from Verse and Prose. A Bird Song, Heart of Oak I., The Secret from Little Flower Folks. What Robin Told, George Cooper; The Nestlings, Laura F. Pollard.

13. The Dandelion — Bright Little Dandelion; The Cherry Tree, Bjornson; The Child and the Apple, Elaine G. Eastman, from the German.

14. Animal Life, pp. 90-93; The Chicken's Mistake, Phoebe Cary.

Number.

Winter.

Begin Number—Teach combinations through six.

(*a*) Addition and subtraction tables 3-6, oral and written.

(*b*) Exact multiplications and divisions—product and dividend not to exceed 6.

(*c*) $\frac{1}{2}$ of 1, 2, 4, and 6; $\frac{1}{3}$ of 1, 3, and 6.

(*d*) Names, figures, and Roman Numerals through six, written.

(*e*) Concrete problems based on Science and Literature.

(*f*) Compound numbers—Liquid measure: 3 feet = 1 yard. $5\frac{1}{2}$ yards = 1 rod. Learned by actual measurement, by the children.

Spring Term.

(a) Review of last term's work.
(b) Addition and subtraction tables through *ten*.
(c) Exact multiplication and division through ten.
(d) $\frac{1}{4}$ of 8 and 10; $\frac{1}{3}$ of 9; $\frac{1}{4}$ of 4 and 8; $\frac{1}{2}$ of 10.
(e) Names of numbers, figures, and Roman numerals 7-10.
(f) Concrete problems drawn from the other studies.
(g) Compound numbers—Dry Measure. 10 cents=one dime, 10 dimes=one dollar; 7 days=1 week, with names of days of week learned in order.
(h) Picturing problems as test of child's understanding.
(i) Rapid addition of single columns of numbers, the sum not to exceed ten.

REMARKS.

The children acquire number facts incidentally in literature, science, reading, and writing, thus: *In Literature:*

1. How many animals did the old woman go to for help? (The class count as one child names them.)
2. How many things did Red Riding Hood take to her grandmother? (2) Show as many fingers as there were trees around the grandmother's house.
8. How many musicians were there in the band?

In Science the number of facts which may be learned without detracting from interest in the subject is great, *e. g.:*

1 (a) Look at the tracks of the dog in the soft earth. How many toe tracks did two feet leave? (b) How many long, sharp teeth has the dog in his two jaws? (c) On how many toe-nails does the cow stand? (d) How many front teeth does the cow lack in the upper jaw?

In Reading: The children may be asked to read three, four, or five lines or more. What is the third word in the second line? etc. Turn to page 12; it looks like this—12 (showing on the board).

In Drawing: Make a border in threes of your leaves; in fours: in fives. How many toes of the chicken can you see? Draw the toes as you see them. Draw the fir tree with six of its brothers and sisters. Draw some little mice running out to get their supper. How many did you draw?

In Writing and Spelling (second term): You may write the word *sheep* three times. How many letters in the word? How many sounds? How many silent letters in *through?* How many letters in the word?

Third Term.

(*a*) A continuation of work as previously suggested for second term. (*f*) Concrete stories based on literature and science given in a number recitation *e.g.*

How many apple blossoms on this twig? (Eight.) You may have four of them, Harry. How many have I left? What part of my blossoms did I give Harry? Give one-half of your blossoms to Nellie. How many has Nellie? Nellie may give one-half of her blossoms to Ruth. Tell me, without speaking, with the chalk, how many apple blossoms I have. How many I gave Harry. What part I gave Harry ($\frac{1}{2}$), etc. Show what I did with my blossoms (8—4), and also how many I have left (8—4=4). Let the chalk tell what part of my blossoms I gave Harry. ($\frac{1}{2}$ of 8), etc. (*h*) Picture *this* at the board. "I bought two quarts of milk at two cents a pint."

Written Language.

(*a*) Short stories—given orally by the children, then written by them. These stories are taken from the literature and nature study. This work is made very easy at first. The children draw pictures on the board of objects, as dictated by the teacher: *e.g.*, of the cow, the teacher writes the word on the board and each child labels his cow. (This work, of course, is very crude at first.) Later they write *The cow,* or *the cow.* They picture a pail of milk, and write the word *milk* below it. After learning to write a number of name words, they write short sentences, as "The cow gives milk," making a picture of the cow giving milk. (b) Copying of short poems or rhymes which they have learned. The children in this grade learn how to begin and end a sentence.

Drawing.

(a) Objects studied in science are drawn by having the object placed before the child, he doing his best to represent it. Some of these objects are molded, as the eggs and nest of the robin, beans and peas in the pod, the horse's shoe, the chicken's foot, cones of the pines. Some are also cut from colored papers and pasted, the children themselves matching the colors, as leaves on the twig of the apple, the ripened fruit of apple, cherry, and plum; beans in the pod.

(b) The stories which the children learn are illustrated by them, they representing on paper what is in their minds, e.g.:

1. They picture the old woman leading her pig, etc.
2. Little Red Riding Hood is represented by them on her way to her grandmother's, meeting the wolf.

Spelling.

(a) Phonetic and written spelling of words needed in the written language. (b) Sentences dictated by the teacher containing these words.

Writing.

(a) Careful writing of the small letters which the children have already learned to write in words in the written language. (b) Combination of these letters into familiar words. (c) Exercises for free movement. Much of the work is done on the board where the letters can be written in a large form. The vertical script is used.

In this work the letters most easily made and commonly used are taught first. Thus i, n, in, m, a, mamma, man, e, men, mine, name, c, mice, nice, nice mamma, o, no, one, one man.

Second Year.

Literature,—Robinson Crusoe.

A Class. First Term. Fall.

Chapters 1-9 in Robinson Crusoe for Boys and Girls.
1. Robinson Crusoe at Home.
2. The Voyage.
3. The Island.
4. Robinson's House.
5. His Work.
6. Surprises. (Wheat found growing in his yard, and a turtle found on the shore.)
7. His sickness.
8. Exploring the Island. (He finds many grapes, melons, oranges, lemons, and cocoanuts.)
9. Another Trip. (He finds a parrot and takes it home for a pet.)

Second Term. Winter.

Chapters 10-20.
10. Robinson's Garden. (He finds salt also.)
11 and 12. Robinson Becomes a Cook.
13. He Becomes a Boatmaker.
14. He Becomes a Tailor.
15. The Second Canoe.
16. Robinson's Flocks.
17. His Manner of Living.
18. Alarm!
19. Robinson Prepares for Trouble.
20. A Discovery.

Third Term. Spring.

Chapters 21-29.
21. Return of the Savages.
22. Making Friday's Acquaintance.
23. Robinson a Teacher.
24. Preparation for a Journey.
25. The Savages' Second Return.
26. A Happy Meeting.
27. Getting Ready for New Guests.
28. An English Vessel Arrives.
29. Home Again.

Nature Study.

First Term. Fall.

Continue and finish the study of *Lima Beans, Sweet Peas,* and *Corn*. Finish study of *Apples* and *Plums* begun the previous spring. *Metamorphosis of cabbage-caterpillar.* If taken at the very beginning of the term, the eggs may be found, and all changes noticed until we have the butterfly. Metamorphosis of milk-weed caterpillar, and other caterpillars which the children may find.

6. (*a*) Wheat: (*b*) Oats (By comparison with wheat); (*c*) The Turtle.

8. (*a*) *Grapes* and *raisins*. (Study of the ripened fruit on the vine.) (*b*) Watermelons and muskmelons studied from flower to mature fruit; (*c*) Orange (As found in market); (*d*) Lemon. (By comparison with the orange.) (The trees of both of the latter will be available to many); (*e*) Cocoanut. (Its manner of growth must be learned from pictures and by comparisons.

Second Term. Winter.

9. (*a*) *Parrot*, if the bird can be seen by the children; (*b*) Crow; Owl (by comparison with the parrot); (*a*) *Snow Crystals*—their history: (*b*) crystals of *salt* and *sulphur;* (*c*) Quartz crystals. Watch for and note time of return of spring birds.

12. (*a*) Watch for pussies on the *willow*. (Robinson made his baskets from twigs of the willow.) Notice the first changes in the buds of this tree and of its mate which bears the seeds. Notice all succeeding changes in both trees. (*b*) Notice, also, the development of the sterile and of the fertile flowers of the *soft maple*, and of its leaf buds. While in the willow the two kinds of flowers are found on separate trees, in the soft maple, the two kinds are found on the same tree. (*c*) Note, likewise, the development of the flower and leaf buds of the elm. Notice difference in shapes between the leaf and flower buds. This tree differs from the two previously studied in having but one kind of flower—a perfect one.

16. (*a*) *Goat*. (By comparison with the sheep, if this has been previously studied.) (*b*) Simple process of butter and cheese making.

Third Term. Spring.

(*a*) Continue the study of the *willow*, *soft maple*, and *elm* until end of term or until the seeds have ripened. (*b*) Sow melon, lemon, orange, and grape seeds. Watch growth and changes. (Continued from autumn.) (*c*) Grapes— buds, blossoms, and green fruits. (Continued from autumn.) (*d*) *Bluebird*—whose arrival has previously been noted. (*e*) *Brown Thrush*—one of our sweetest summer songsters. (*f*) *Violet*. (*g*) *Morning Glory*. [The order in which these plants and birds shall be taken up for study will be determined largely by the time of their arrival.]

BOOKS FOR REFERENCE.

Wheat and other grains, and bread making. (*a*) Cyclopedia of Common Things, pp. 648, 87, 584. (*b*) Stories of Industry II., pp. 82-97. (*c*) Story of a Grain of Wheat, St. Nicholas, Oct., 1893. (*d*) Flour Mills of Minneapolis. Century May, 1886.

Salt. (*a*) Piece of Rock Salt, "Science for All," Vol. II., p. 279. (*b*) Cyclopedia of Common Things, pp. 528, 201, 529.

Crystals. (a) Shaler's First Book in Geology. (b) Cyclopedia of Common Things, pp. 497, 518, 572.

Parrot. (a) Cyclopedia of Common Things, pp. 444 and 445. (b) Anderson-Maskel "Children With the Birds," p. 265. (c) Johnnot's "Wings and Fins," p. 221. (d) Standard Natural History, Vol. 4., p. 349. (e) Johnson's Natural History, Vol. 2 (see index for page). (f) Museum of Natural History, Vol. 2 (see index for page).

Crow. (a) "Wake Robin." p. 111. (b) "Little Brothers of the Air," p. 236. (c) Standard Natural History, Vol. 4 (see index). (d) Wilson's "American Ornithology," Vol. 2, p. 80. (e) "North American Birds," Baird, Vol. 2, p. 243. (f) Northern and Eastern Birds," Samuels, p. 357.

Spring Birds. (a) Burrough's Wake Robin." (b) Olive Thorne Miller's "In Nesting Time." (c) Keyser's "Birddom." See also any good book of Ornithology or an Encyclopedia.

Tree Blossoms. (a) Mrs. Dyson's "Stories of the Trees." (b) Apgar's "Trees of Northern United States." (c) Gray's Structural and Physiological Botanies. (d) Newell's Outlines of Lessons in Botany, Vols. I. and II.

Reading.

First Term. Fall.

(a) Story of The Straw, the Coal of Fire, and the Bean, in Classic Stories for the Little Ones. (b) The Child and the Apple, Elaine G. Eastman. The Peasant and the Apple Tree, Æsop. (c) Nature stories for Young Readers, Part II, pp. 69-71, 78-81, 108-110, 153-156. Cat Tails and Other Tales, 35-41, 88-93. (d) Nature Stories II, 35-38.

5. The Lamp, Æsop (Robinson makes a lamp).

6. The Hare and the Tortoise, The Tortoise and the Eagle, Æsop.

8. The Vine and the Goat, The Fox and the Grapes, The

Hart and the Vine. Æsop. Hodskin's Little People's Reader, pp. 52-92.

Second Term. Winter.
Classic Stories, VII-X.

9. The Crow and the Pitcher, The Crow and the Sheep, Æsop. The Crow's Children, Alice Cary. The Pigeon and the Owl, Emilie Poulsson. The Bird With No Name, Classic Stories. Owl, Nature Stories II.

10. Snowflakes, Nature Stories I. The Vapor Family, What the Fire Sprites Did, How Dame Nature Got Her Frost, Who Broke the China Pitcher, A Vapor Story, from Cat Tails and Other Tales. Jack Frost, Poem.

11. Grandma Kaoline, in Cat Tails and Other Tales. How the Indians Learned to Make Clay Dishes, Nature Myths. Address to a Robin.

12. Pussy Willow, Sugar Making, from Nature Stories I. Pussy Willow's Hood, in Cat Tails and Other Tales. Young March Wind, M. F. Butts. Pussy Willow, Mary E. Plummer in Kindergarten Magazine. "O, You Pussy Willow," Poem. Talking in their Sleep, Edith M. Thomas in St. Nicholas.

16. Little One Eye, The Wolf and the Goat, from Scudder's Fables and Folk Lore. Grimms' Fairy Tales, Wiltse.

Third Term. Spring.

(*a*) Maple Seeds, Nature Stories I. (*b*) The Little Brown Seed, Cat Tails and Other Tales. The Wind and the Sun, Æsop. A Cloud Story, Phaeton, Nature Myths. Spring Rain, Nature Stories I. Poems—Rain and the Flowers; Who Likes the Rain, Clara Doty Bates: How Queer, Robert Louis Stevenson. (*d* and *e*) Mr. and Mrs. Robin, Cat Tails and Other Tales. Spring News, Nature Stories I. The Cat and the Birds, The Lark and Her Young Ones, from Æsop. (*f*) Violet, (*g*) Dandelion, from Nature Stories I. Poems—Bright Little Dandelion: Dandelion, dandelion, where's your cap of gold? The Proud Apple Branch, the Pea Blossom, The Ugly Duckling, from Classic Stories. Cyr's Second Reader. Morning Glory—a poem.

Number.

Fall Term—(*a*) Addition and subtraction tables through 13. (*b*) Addition of single columns of numbers, sum not exceeding 13. (*c*) Recognition of all numbers up to 100 as composed of tens and units. (*d*) Addition of two-place numbers, the sum of no column to exceed nine—thus

$$\begin{array}{r} 22 \\ 36 \\ 21 \\ \hline 79 \end{array}$$

(*e*) Subtraction in two-place numbers where no figure in the subtrahend exceeds the corresponding figure in the minuend—thus

$$\begin{array}{r} 97 \\ 46 \\ \hline 51 \end{array}$$

(*f*) Multiplication table of 10's. (*g*) two 6's, six 2's, three 4's, four 3's, 12÷2's, 3's, 4's, and 6's. (*h*) Fractions ½ of all numbers 1 to 13. Illustrate with objects. (*i*) Figures from 1 to 100. (*j*) Measurements—Liquid Measure, Dry Measure, Time Tables reviewed. (*k*) Concrete problems from Literature and Science. (*l*) Picturing problems—as 5 pints=2 quarts and 1 pint.

Winter Term—1. (*a*) Of last term continued through 17.

2. Review of (*b*) 5½ yards=1 rod. Work continued through 17.

3. Review (*c*), (*d*), and (*e*), in work of fall term.

4. Review multiplication table 10's. Take in advance table 5's.

5. Review all multiplications and divisions taken. Advance through 17.
  6. Review (*h*). Continue through 17.
  $\frac{1}{2}$ of 1, 3, 6, 9, 12, 15.
  $\frac{1}{4}$ of 1, 4, 8, 12, 16.
  $\frac{1}{5}$ of 1, 5, 10, 15.
  $\frac{1}{6}$ of 1, 6, 12.
  $\frac{1}{7}$ of 1, 7, 14.
  $\frac{1}{8}$ of 1, 8, 16.
  $\frac{1}{9}$ of 1, 9.
  $\frac{1}{10}$ of 1, 10.
  7. Review (*i*).
  8. Review (*j*). Review table of U. S. money; first three facts in Long Measure, Liquid, and Dry Measures.
  9. Continue (*k*).
  10. Continue (*l*).

Hall's Arithmetic Reader, pp. 47-95, excepting work not called for in the above.

Spring Term.

1. Continue work as outlined above through 20.
2. Review all work previously taken.
3. Forty-five facts in addition fixed.
4. Much addition of single columns of numbers (sum not to exceed one hundred), by grasping the tens.
5. Multiplication table of 2's.

Remarks.

Much of this work is based on Nature Study and the story of Robinson Crusoe: the story brings into use the tables of long measure, liquid and dry measures, and the time table. The children measure off on the school yard the distance from the door of Robinson's cave to his fence in front, the distance apart of the ends of his fence, which was in the form of a semi-circle, the length and breadth of his cabin. In cutting out his clothes the different pieces are measured. His baskets held different amounts; his jars also. He measures his milk, his wheat, and rice; he gathers lemons, oranges, and cocoanuts by the dozen. The number of goats in his different pastures are made the basis of study. In nature study the number of beans and of peas in a pod, the number of rows of corn on a cob, the number of ears of corn on a stalk, of stalks in a hill, the distance apart of the hills, etc., furnish material for the number work, and at the same time help to a clearer idea of the object studied. The number of plums in a quart; of medium-sized apples in a peck. The distance around a large apple or plum; through it, also. The number of grapes in a bunch, counted. Size of grapes. Number of seeds in a grape. Length of full grown pussies. Length of sprays of seed. Size of watermelon and muskmelon. Number of melons on some vines. Number of petals in a flower. Number of points on a crystal, etc.

Written Language.

(a) Stories from Robinson Crusoe and Nature Study given by the children as in first year. (b) In addition to the points emphasized in first grade, the children learn to paragraph. (c) Copying of poems learned by them, as in first grade. (d) Writing of short letters in good form.

Writing.

(a) Careful making of capital letters already used in Written Language, and such others as will be used through the year. (b) Familiar words beginning with capital letters. (c) Exercises for free movement as before. (d) Writing of stanzas of poems which the children have learned, using the capital letters with which they are working.

Spelling.

(a) Words needed for the Written Language, spelled phonetically and written. (b) Sentences dictated by the teacher containing these words. (c) Words of more than one syllable are properly divided and spelled orally by syllable.

Drawing.

As in first grade.

Poems for Memorizing in First Grade.

Fall Term.

1. "One Little Cloud."
2. "Cricket Song." E. Whitney.
3. "The Wind."
4. "The Sunbeams."
5. "Lady Moon." Lord Houghton.
6. "Windy Nights." Robert Louis Stevenson.
7. "Jack Frost."
8. "Snowflakes."
9. "The First Christmas." Emilie Poulsson.

Songs.

1. "Where Do All the Daisies Go?" Child's Song Book.
2. "Fly Away." Kindergarten Mag., Nov., '91.
3. "Come Little Leaves." Child's Song Book.
4. "Jack Frost." Merry Songs and Games.
5. "O, There is a Little Artist." Child's Song Book.
6. "O, Mother, How Pretty the Moon Looks." Merry Songs and Games.
7. "Rap! Rap! Rap!" Dainty Songs.
8. "I'm a Little Sunbeam." Infant Praises.
9. "The Pop Corn Song." Child's Song Book.
10. "Little Gay Bunny Coat." Child's Song Book."
11. "The Sleigh Song." The Golden Boat.

12. "The Snowflakes." Songs for Little Children II.
13. "Merry Christmas Bells." Dainty Songs.
14. "Christmas Hymn." Kindergarten Chimes.
Opening and closing songs, as given in Winter plan.

Poems for Memorizing in First Grade.
Winter Term.

1. "The Snow," Peasley's Graded Selections.
2. Snowflakes ("Tap, tap, tap, what a tiny call," Review.)
3. Jack Frost (in review.)
4. The Ferns (Oh what shall we do the long winter through.)
5. The Little Chickadees.
6. Pine Needles. Wm. Hayne.
7. Kitty in the Basket. Mrs. Follen.
8. One Little Cloud (in review.)
9. Washington (Only a Babe). Emilie Poulsson.
10. Spring Cleaning. Thos. Tapper.
11. March (Oh, March, why are you scolding?)
12. Young March Wind. M. F. Butts.
13. The Wind. (I am the Wind) (in review.)
14. Windy Nights. Robert Louis Stevenson (in review).
15. Address to a Robin.

Morning Songs.

1. "Heavenly Father, May We Know All the Way Our Feet Should Go," School Songs A.
2. "Father in Heaven Help Thy Little Children," Kindergarten Chimes.
3. "Father Help Each Little Child," Mrs. Hailmann's Songs, Games, and Rhymes.
4. "Father, We Thank Thee for the Night," Songs and Games, Walker & Jenks.

Songs.

1. This is the Way the Snow Comes Down." Dainty Songs.
2. "Little Miss Snowflake." The Child's Song Book.
3. "Oh, See the Snow!" Mrs. Hailmann's Songs, Games, and Rhymes.
4. "Away, Away, the Track is White," Forest Choir.
5. Jack Frost (in review). "Merry Songs and Games. I. Hubbard.
6. O, There is a Little Artist that Paints in the Cold Night Hours (in review). The Child's Song Book.
7. "Twinkle, Twinkle, Little Star." Infant Praises.
8. "Oh, Mother, How Pretty the Moon Looks!" (in review). Merry Songs and Games.
9. "Good Morning, Merry Sunshine." Merry Songs and Games.
10. "Merry Little Sunbeams." The Child's Song Book.
11. "Hurrah for the Flag." The Child's Song Book.
12. Rap! Rap! Rap! (in review). Dainty Songs.
13. "I'm a Little Sunbeam" (in review). Infant Praises.
14. "Three Little Kittens" (in review). The Child's Song Book.
15. The Pop Corn Song (in review). The Child's Song Book.
16. When the Little Children Sleep. Kindergarten Chimes.
17. Little Gay Bunny Coat (in review). The Child's Song Book.
18. Wynken, Blynken, and Nod. Riverside Song Book.

Closing Songs.

(a) "Now Our Morning Work is Ended." "Merry Songs and Games," Hubbard.

(b) Good Night. The Child's Song Book.

For the Second Grade.

(c) Farewell Work and Farewell Play. Songs, Games, and Rhymes.

Games.

1. The Pigeon Song (in review). Songs for Little Folks. Crafts & Merrill.
2. (a) Merrily, Merrily let us Form a Ring (in review). (b) Tramp! Tramp! Tramp! (in review). Merry Songs and Games I.
3. Hop, Little Rabbit. The Child's Song Book.
4. Come Take a Little Partner (in review). Merry Songs and Games.

Poems for Memorizing in First Grade.

Spring Term.

1. "A Little Brown Seed."
2. "The Nestlings." Laura F. Pollard.
3. "One Little Cloud." (Review.)
4. "Who Stole the Bird's Nest." Lydia Maria Child.
5. "The Chicken's Mistake." Phœbe Cary.
6. "The Dandelion." "Peaslee's Graded Selections."
7. "The Wind." (Review.)
8. "The Secret." "Little Flower Folks."
9. "What Robin Told." Geo. Cooper in "Little Flower Folks."
10. "Dimple and Rosy Wing." Annette Bishop.
11. "Cricket Songs." E. Whitney in St. Nicholas, December 1886.
12. "Pine Needles." (Review) Wm. H. Hayne in St. Nicholas, February, 1887.
13. "The Grass Blades."
14. "Rain Drops."
15. "How Queer." Robert Louis Stevenson.

Songs.

Opening songs as last term.
1. "Queer Little House." "The Child's Song Book."
2. "Robin's Lullaby" Stories in Song.
3. "In the Tall Boughs." Stories in Song.
4. "Reminding the Hen." Hanson's Calisthenic Songs.
5. "Jolly Little Clacker." Forest Choir.
6. "Hark! Buzz! Hum!" The Child's Song Book.
7. "The Violet." Songs and Games for Little Ones.
8. "The Raindrop's Song." "Golden Boat."
9. "Drip! Drip! Drip" The Child's Song Book.
10. "When the Rain Comes Down." The Child's Song Book.
11. "Oh, say where do you come from?" School Songs A.
12. "The Tree Song." "The Golden Boat."
13. "Finger Song." "Songs for Little Children," II.
14. "I'm a Little Sunbeam." "Infant Praises."
15. "Rock-a-bye-baby." "The Child's Song Book."
16. "When Little Birdie bye-bye goes." "Songs, Games, and Rhymes."
17. "Wynken, Blynken, and Nod." Riverside Song Book.
18. "A Song for Summer." "Stories in Song."
Closing songs as last term.

Games.

1. "The Dollies Dance." "Golden Boat."
2. "The Tip-toe Song." "Golden Boat."
3. "The Snail." "Songs, Games, and Rhymes."

Poems for Memorizing in Second Grade.
Fall Term.

1. "The Sunbeams." Emilie Poulsson.
2. "The Aster."

For the Second Grade.

3. "Golden Rod."
4. "September." H. H.
5. "Who Likes the Rain?" Clara Doty Bates.
6. "Friends." L. G. Warner.
7. "Old Squirrel Gray."
8. "How the Leaves Came Down." Susan Coolidge.
9. "The Pine Tree's Secret. Emilie Poulsson.
10. "A Night with a Wolf." Bayard Taylor.
11. "Thanksgiving."
12. "Christmas Eve." Mary Mapes Dodge.
13. "The Mountain and the Squirrel." Emerson.

Songs.

1. "Grasshopper Green. Songs and Games.
2. "Buzz! Buzz! Buzz!" Dainty Songs.
3. "The Raindrop's Song." The Golden Boat.
4. "Song of Bells." The Golden Boat.
5. "The Tip-Toe Song." The Golden Boat.
6. "The Pigeon House." Stories in Song.
7. "November." Riverside Song Book.
8. "When the Little Children Sleep." Kindergarten Chimes.
9. "The Shoemaker." Songs for Little Children II.
10. "The Wonderful Weaver." Stories in Song.
11. "Sleighing Song." Dainty Songs.
12. "Kris Kringle." Riverside Song Book.
13. "Luther's Cradle Hymn." Dainty Songs.
14. "Christmas Tree March." Kindergarten Chimes.

Poems for Memorizing in Second Grade.
Winter Term.

1. The Moon ("Oh Moon, said the Children.").
2. The Sunbeams. Emile Poulsson. (In review.)
3. Jack Frost. (In review.)

4. Snowflakes. (Whenever a snowflake leaves the sky.)
5. The Ferns.
6. February Twenty-second.
7. March (Wordsworth.)
8. Young March Wind. M. F. Butts.
9. Pussy Willow.

Songs.

Opening songs. (See First Grade.)

1. White Lambkins. Mrs. Hailmann's Songs, Games, and Rhymes.
2. Twinkle, Twinkle, Little Star. Infant Praises.
3. Jack Frost. Songs, Games, and Rhymes.
4. Away, Away, the Track is White, Forest Choir.
5. Oh, There is a Little Artist (in review). The Child's Song Book.
6. The Song of the Snowbird. Hanson's Calisthenic Songs.
7. Chickadee. Forest Choir.
8. The Snow Bird. School Songs A.
9. "Polly." Merry Songs and Games.
10. America.
11. Washington's Birthday. Forest Choir.
12. The Pop Corn Song. The Child's Song Book.
13. "When the Little Children Sleep" (in review) Kindergarten Chimes.
14. "Tic! Tic!" Forest Choir.
15. Wynken, Blynken, and Nod (in review). Riverside Song Book.
16. Pretty Pussies Down by the Brook. The Child's Song Book.
17. I know the Song that the Bluebird is Singing. Songs and Games. Walker & Jenks.

Closing Songs.

"Now Our Morning Work is Ended." Merry Songs and Games.

Good Night." Forest Choir.

"Now the Busy Day is Over." Songs and Games. Walker & Jenks.

Games.

Same as in First Primary, excepting "Hop, Little Rabbit."

Poems for Memorizing in Second Grade.

Spring Term.

1. "Rain and the Flowers."
2. "The Cherry Tree." Bjornson.
3. "Flowers and Weeds." Geo. Cooper.
4. "Dandelion."
5. "April's Answer to a Child." Mary F. Butts.
6. Japanese Lullaby.
7. "Over in the Meadow." Olive A. Wadsworth.
8. "Discontent." Sarah O. Jewett.
9. "Morning Glory."

Songs.

1. "To and Fro." Stories in Song.
2. "To Mother Farie." Riverside Song Book.
3. "The Farmer." Songs for Little Children.
4. "The Little Mothers." Hanson's Calesthenic Songs.
5. "The Rain Shower." Songs for Little Children II.
6. "A Song for Summer." Stories in Song.
7. "Millions of Tiny Raindrops." Forest Choir.
8. "When the Rain Comes Down." Child's Song Book.
9. "Little White Lily." Songs for Little Children II.

10. "Dandelion Fashions." Songs for Little Children II.
11. "Violet." Kindergarten Chimes.
12. "Bee Song." Forest Choir.
13. "In the Tall Boughs." Stories in Song.
14. "Birdies in the Greenwood." Songs, Games, and Rhymes.
15. "Bob White." Child's Song Book.
16. "Little Brown Thrush." Merry Songs and Games.
17. "There's a Little Bird's Nest." Infant Praises.

Third Grade.

Introduction.

Let the teacher of each class make a study of all the work done by the third grade in different branches. The relations of the branches to each other will thus become apparent. In the effort to associate and concentrate studies keep in mind (1) All the studies of the entire year. One term's work in natural science $e.\,g.$ does not stand alone, but is related to the work of the preceding term and to what follows. It depends often, also, upon geography or history. (2) Gather in, in all lessons, the home experiences of children (apperception) with which to illustrate and explain new topics, and give them greater interest and closer connection with life. (3) The application of knowledge gained in one study to other studies and to new lessons is the best use that can be made of it.

The time given to each study is as follows: Reading, every day; arithmetic, daily; spelling, daily; literature or history alternates with natural science, each coming every other day; geography alternates with language lessons; drawing alternates with writing.

Reading.

First Term. Fall.

1. Scudder's Fables and Folk Lore, pp. 81–103.
2. Fairy Tales in Verse, pp. 109–136; pp. 160–169, and Prose Selections (Rolfe).
3. Open Sesame No. I. Selections.
4. Thanksgiving and poems of nature.

5. A Christmas Carol.
6. The Children of the Wood (Wiggin).
7. The Story of Christmas.
8. The First Thanksgiving Day (The Story Hour).

Study chapters 2 and 6 of Special Method in Reading. Phonic drill on vowel sounds, with marking.

Second Term. Winter.

Finish Fables and Folk Lore. Read Robinson Crusoe for Boys and Girls. Illustrate with pictures and connect with excursions in home geography. Andersen's Fairy Tales, Part I. For sight reading. Golden Book of choice reading, for occasional use. Memory selections from Open Sesame, Vol. I. Phonic drill on sonants and non-sonants.

Third Term. Spring.

Continue Andersen's Fairy Tales, No. I. Heart of Oak, No. II. For sight reading use Æsop's Fables. Wiggins' Froebel's Birthday (April 21); also The Oriole's Nest. Select pieces from Open Sesame, Vol. I. Complete phonic drill with markings. Study the Special Method in Reading for suggestion.

Arithmetic.

First Term. Fall.

Thorough review of tables in addition, subtraction, and multiplication, through 20. Addition of columns of two place numbers, of three place numbers. Fractions, $\frac{1}{2}, \frac{1}{3}, \frac{1}{4}, \frac{1}{5}$ of all numbers to 20. Illustrate with objects and paper folding. Read numbers to 1,000. Explain and Illustrate the decimal scale. Roman numeration to 20. Cook and Cropsey pp. 164.

Study Cook's Methods in Written Arithmetic for suggestion and advice in correctness in language, forms of explanation, variety and form of board exercises, oral drills, etc.

For the Third Grade. 41

Variety of object work and graphic board work by teacher and pupil is needed. Dispense with the objects as soon as the thought is clear. Learn to think and picture numbers clearly before writing.

Second Term.   Winter.

Read and write numbers to 5,000: Roman numerals to 500. Review denominate numbers of second grade. Add columns of three place numbers. Subtract three and four place numbers not above 5,000. Find half of all numbers from 12 to 50. Multiplication tables of 10's, 5's, 2's, 4's, 8's, and 3's. Rapid and frequent oral drill in addition and subtraction. The order of tables is significant.

Notice the subjects treated in geography, natural science, and other studies, and see if good, concrete problems in number are furnished. The excursions in geography supply opportunity to measure distances and buildings, to examine weights and measures. Compound numbers are illustrated by the sale of things by the dozen, pound, foot, yard, quart, bushel, bunch, basket, box, etc.

Third Term.   Spring.

Arabic notation and numeration through six orders. Multiplication tables of 6's, 9's, and 7's with complete review of previous tables. Multiply with multipliers of not more than three figures. Short division with divisors up to 10. Long division with divisors not more than 25.

Complete the object work for tables of dry measure, liquid measure, long measure, and United States Money. Apply this knowledge of numbers to the simple reductions in these tables from one denomination to another.

Study and measure the sphere, hemisphere, ovoid, cube, and prism.

Geography.

First Term. Fall.

Excursions to a house in process of building, lumber yard, planing mill, tinner's, brick kiln. Visit to a gardener, fall vegetables and fruits, canning factory, fruit store, grocery, the farmer's harvest, the nursery, packing, etc. Visit to the cupola of the Normal building, views of prairie, forest, city, town, slopes of fields, etc., the campus with its slopes and drainage, the streams, brooks, and bridges near town. Visit to Miller's Park, notice creek, valley, hills and slopes. All excursions described and discussed systematically in class, the topics arranged into series and in each child's outline book in ink. A map of the campus in sand should be made. The map of campus and town, with a few leading roads, should be drawn to a scale. Consult chapter I of Special Method in Geography. Recitations on alternate days.

Second Term. Winter.

Boiler house and heating apparatus, furnaces, coal and wood as fuel, where obtained. Feed mill, engine, cornsheller, bins, kinds of grain, feeding stock on the farms in winter. School house garret, framework and timbers. The green-house, kinds of plants, soils. Ice-packing, ponds, ice-houses. Shipping goods at the freight office, railroad commerce, station agent, foreign products, as fruits, coffee, tea, sugar, dry goods, and where they come from. Foreign countries, the earth as a whole, illustrated by globes and pictures, the continents and oceans. Cause of day and night. Seven Little Sisters, read in selections. Local history and management of the town, the council, streets, police. All important topics carefully reproduced and outlines preserved in outline books. Many objects seen should be sketched on blackboard or on paper.

Third Term. Spring.

Gardens, hot-beds, farmer's spring work. The nursery, tree planting, shipping. The streams in the spring time, rains, and floods. Water works, engines, pipes, fountains. The court house, records, vaults, officers, court room, trials. Blacksmith's shop, the tinner's, hardware, the machine shops (railroad), carriage works, stove foundry. A carpet weaver, woolen mill, dry goods, etc. Churches, theatres, parks, monuments with history. Electric light plants, street car lines, railroads and neighboring towns. Draw map. The list of various industries in the town and neighborhood. Division of labor. One spring excursion to some more distant place of interest, as Mackinaw Dells (20 miles). Discuss and reproduce all important topics. Locate Illinois on the map of the world.

Literature.

First Term. Fall.

1. The Miraculous Pitcher.
2. The Paradise of Children.
3. The Three Golden Apples.
4. The Golden Touch.
5. The Gorgon's Head.
6. The Pygmies.

Oral presentation of the stories, clear, simple, and vivid. Use good pictures to illustrate the ancient stories. Pictures of some of the standard works of art will help greatly.

Get full and clear reproductions from the children. Watch the language and quietly correct mistakes in English. At first outlines will greatly help both teacher and pupils in clear and definite grasp. But do not allow the outlines to grow into mechanical and formal habit.

Stories taken chiefly from the Wonder Book of Hawthorne.

Second Term. Winter.

1. The Minotaur.
2. The Dragon's Teeth.
3. Circe's Palace.
4. The Pomegranate Seed.
5. The Golden Fleece.
6. The Story of Ulysses.
7. The Chimæra.

Stories mostly from Hawthorne's Tanglewood Tales. Other excellent books are Kingsley's Greek Heroes, Gods and Heroes, and Stories of the Old World. The geography of Greece and the seas will help to give meaning or location to some of the stories. A little comparative study of these myths in different books will help the teachers. Let the children's imagination develop healthfully on these stories. Use good pictures from books in the library. Occasionally written tests may be of value. Put difficult words on the board and give a class drill upon them. Keep outlines of the stories. Let each child preserve the outlines in his blank-book.

Third Term. Spring.

1. Lamb's Adventures of Ulysses.
2. Church's Story of the Iliad.
3. Use for comparison.
4. Macmillan's Story of the Odyssey and Story of the Iliad.

Good, illustrative pictures may be had in the library. Let the moral judgment of the children be developed in estimating the characters and their deeds. Use the geography of the stories when it is clear. Good class attention is indispensable in this oral instruction. Hold the children responsible for free, full, and accurate reproductions. Keep the characters distinct, and do not mix the stories and scenes. Keep outlines for review and reference.

In the Special Method in Literature and History, study the chapters on Greek Myths and Pioneer History Stories, especially the oral method of treatment.

Natural Science.

First Term. Fall.

The sunflower, life, history, its kindred. The thistle, its seeds, compared with other compositae in fall. The goldenrod. The corn plant, history, parts, uses. The blue grass and other grasses. Wheat and other grains. The potato, the tomato, the melons. The apple tree, age and growth, fruit. The oak, acorns, gall nuts, leaves and changes in the fall; compare with nut-bearing trees. Grasshoppers, food, what becomes of them. The north star, position, compare with other stars. The sun, movements, length of day, the calendar, time table. Frost, temperature, thermometers, effect of frost and cold on vegetation. The crow, his flight, food, rookeries. Clay, sand, soils, collected from several places.

A few class excursions are necessary. Plants and observations collected by children should be discussed and worked over.

Second Term. Winter.

Continue the observations of the fall term on trees, the crow, experiments with soils, cold and thermometers, the sun and its changes. Snow crystals, ice, effects of cold and heat. The big dipper, its movements. The rabbit, winter food, care of rabbits. The sheep, wool, winter clothing of animals. The snow birds, how they live, canaries. Geraniums and begonias (hot house). The coffee plant, its home in warm countries. The beaver, the seal, their icy home. The hard maple, preparations for spring, the sap in February, vaporization, boiling away water, steam, vapor, clouds, rain. Iron as a metal, ore, melting, compare with lead, compare with gold and silver.

Encourage children to observe at home, point out times and opportunities for observation. Discuss their real observations in class. Look ahead for materials of study. Arrange all collections in order; use them, and point out other related things.

Third Term. Spring.

Continue certain topics begun in fall and winter. Try to tell what plants in spring come from seeds studied in the fall (sun-flower, thistle, grasses, potato and tomato). Continue the study of the apple tree and oak. Continue the study of the maple, leaves, blossoms, seeds, seedlings. Notice soils and localities in spring. Follow the sun in its changes back to summer.

The robin and the woodpecker. Return of the birds, nesting, rearing the young, food, etc. The spring beauty, place, compare with other wild flowers. The peas and the pea blossoms, vines, pods. The strawberry, blossom, fruit, compare. The rabbit in spring time, care of young. The onion, sets, seeds. The crayfish, habits, life, home, food. The minnows and fishes. Select and plant a tree on arbor day; care of it.

The excursions in geography and science will furnish much material. Plan carefully, study the Special Method in Natural Science for suggestion.

Books of Reference for Science Lessons in third Grade.

Animal Memoirs: Part I., Mammals; Part II., Birds; by Dr. Lockwood. Iveson, Blakeman & Co., Chicago.

How to Study Plants, by A. Wood. A. S. Barnes & Co.

A Year with the Trees, by Wilson Flagg. Educational Pub. Co., Boston.

My Saturday with a Bird Class, by Mary Miller. D. C. Heath & Co., Chicago.

The Succession of Forest Trees and Wild Apples, by Thoreau. Houghton Mifflin & Co., Chicago.

Birds and Bees, by Burroughs. Houghton Mifflin & Co.

The Oak, by Ward. D. Appleton & Co., New York.

The Great World's Farm, by Gage. Seeley & Co., (Macmillan).

Seaside and Wayside, No. III. and IV. D. C. Heath & Co.

The Beauties of Nature, by Lubbock. Macmillan & Co., New York.

Outline Lessons in Botany, Part II., by Newell; and A Reader in Botany, Part I., by Newell. Ginn & Co., Chicago.

Guides for Science Teaching.—First Lessons in Minerals XIII.; Worms and Crustacea VII. D. C. Heath & Co., Chicago.

Stories of the Trees, by Mrs. Dyson.

Trees of Northern United States, by Apgar.

These books will greatly help the teacher in showing points of interest and what to look for, but they can not take the place of close and constant observation.

Language.

The purpose is to secure correct use (oral and written) of good English. There are two sets of exercises.

(1) Oral drills on those words and forms of expression which are difficult or commonly misused, as irregular verbs, pronouns, singular and plural of verb forms, adverbs, comparisons, homonyms, abbreviated forms, colloquial errors and faults in usage, bad pronunciations, wrong accent, varieties of singular and plural forms. Some simple rules may be developed to help in the mastery of these difficulties.

(2) Composition, letters, board and seat exercises to cultivate the use of correct forms in writing, including spelling, punctuation, paragraphing, indenting, use of capitals, abbreviations, titles, addresses, signatures, etc. In letter-writing, aim at neatness and correctness in writ-

ing, and the power of original expression and natural use of good English in composition.

Once in two weeks there should be at least one composition, corrected, revised, and entered for permanent keeping in the outline book. If the first copy is good enough, let a choice verse or selection be copied in the outline book instead.

The oral exercises should be quick, lively, and energetic. In the sentence work the teacher's forethought and plan should supply thought material of value, and involving the use of the verbal forms to be drilled upon. Avoid meaningless and silly sentences. Bright's little language book gives an excellent collection of irregular verbs, homonyms, etc., distributed through the grades as an outline for study. DeGarmo's language books suggest much variety of interesting thought exercises in language drills.

First Term. Fall.

Two lessons out of five should be devoted to written composition. The topics may be drawn from the outlines of literature, geography, and natural science. The children should be observed closely in their written work, errors prevented by preliminary suggestion and advice. The papers should be written with ink on quarter sheets of foolscap and handed in for correction. Papers needing rewriting should be copied in the outline book. For exercise in use of correct English, drills, and board work use Bright, p. 1-18. Also De Garmo, No. II. Exercise great care in capitals, punctuation, writing, and spelling.

The language teacher should keep in close touch with the work in all the other studies of the grade, so as to utilize better in language lessons the thought materials thus furnished.

Second Term. Winter.

Continue composition work as in the fall. The compositions in part should be put in the form of letters, with the explanations, forms, and drills needed. Master the work of Bright in second grade and part of third grade. Use De Garmo's Language work for suggestions as to method, first and second part of No. II. It is well to gather up the colloquial forms in use on the play ground and in the community and drill upon the correct usage. This relates school exercises to life.

Teachers in other studies of the same grade should everywhere, persistently and quietly, enforce correct usage in the classes and even outside the classes. But corrections in language should be made in such a gentle way as not to disturb the free expression of thought.

Third Term. Spring.

Continue the composition exercises. By preserving the written compositions through the year we can mark the progress of the children or their failure to improve in neatness, correctness, and power of written expression of thought. Many of the compositions will be rewritten in the outline books, others may be preserved in the original form. Teachers and parents can look over this work and see approximately the excellence and defects of a child's work and plan better for the future.

Complete Bright's work for the third year. Keep up the applications of first and second year exercises so that children may not drop back again into incorrect usage. Use De Garmo's No. II. parts 2 and 3 for suggestive exercises.

Drawing.

The purpose of Drawing in third and fourth grades is chiefly to contribute to a better grasp of the other studies. The objects drawn will be largely, though not entirely, from those studied in the other subjects. Some sketching may be appropriately done in immediate connection with the recitations in those studies, as in natural science and geography, in reading and arithmetic.

But the more careful work should be done in the drawing hour. As the simple objects are drawn, the corrections and suggestions of the teacher as to form, proportion, and use of materials, may gradually lead up to a grasp and use of the principles underlying the art of drawing.

The teacher, therefore, can afford to examine the range of objects coming up in the third and fourth grades, selecting such as are not too difficult, appropriate to the season, and suitable as drawing lessons.

The plan and course of study outlined by Miss Gertrude A. Stoker, of St. Paul, in her "Seeing and Doing," is recommended to teachers.

First Term. Fall.

Clay modeling and drawing of leaves, fruits, and vegetables, as burdock, sunflower, apple, potato, tomato, pumpkin, squash, and melon. Also grasshoppers, birds, rabbits, butterflies, cow, horse, crow, elm tree, oak, corn plant, wheat, thistle, apple tree.

Second Term. Winter.

Pictures illustrating stories, as boats, streams, mountains, sheep, snow bird, evergreens, trees in winter, the beaver, seal, boxes, chairs, sleds.

Third Term. Spring.

Color studies with flowers and birds. Robin, woodpecker, seedling maple, spring beauty, marsh marigold, pea, strawberry, the minnow, the clam, crayfish.

Writing.

The following suggestions for writing are mainly from Mr. E. W. Cavins, of the Normal School.

Vertical Writing.

To learn vertical writing first learn its *characteristics*.
1. Simplicity and legibility.

2. Letters well developed and well rounded.
3. Stem and loop letters shortened.
4. Initial strokes of many letters omitted.
5. Capitals small and simple.

Pupils may get the desire to learn vertical writing by noticing its advantages over the sloping system.
1. More easily learned.
2. More easily read.
3. Takes less space.
4. Position for writing is more healthful.

It is certainly simple and more definite.

The teacher should

1. Observe order and system in (*a*) seating pupils, (*b*) materials used, (*c*) distributing and collecting materials, (*d*) classifying and presenting subject matter, (*e*) practice work of pupils.

2. Be clear and definite. (*a*) Strike at the essential points. (*b*) One at a time. (*c*) Show what to do. (*d*) And how to do it.

3. Get results (*a*) in neatness, (*b*) in order and spacing, (*c*) on the special point under consideration.

The lower case letters should be practiced first as i, u, w, v, x, n, m, e, r, s, o, c. a, d, g, q, t, p, l, b, h, k, f, j, y, z.

Later the capitals should be practiced, as C, O, D, E, A —N, M, U, V, W, Y, X, Q, Z, H, K—I, J, T, F, L, S, G, P, B, R.

In third grade if the lower case letters have been practiced in lower grades, they can be reviewed, or if not, drill upon them first. Specialize on one letter at a time and on groups of similar letters. For general exercises write words and sentences involving both capitals and small letters.

The writing teacher should notice whether the children apply their writing in composition, spelling, and other studies. The teachers in the other branches also should notice and apply the writing teachers' prescriptions.

Spelling.

The spelling lessons are derived from the other studies of the class in reading, arithmetic, language lessons, geography, natural science, and literature. Each pupil teacher in one of these studies files on the room-teacher's desk a list of from ten to twenty-five words each Monday morning. Ten words are written in ink at each lesson in Sherwood's Writing Speller. Every fifth lesson is a review. Misspelled words are corrected and drilled upon. Some of the simple rules of spelling should be developed from illustrative words, also reviewed and applied till they become useful in practice. The spelling lesson usually takes ten or fifteen minutes just after the opening exercise in the morning. Let teachers insist upon neatness and care in writing. Pronounce words correctly and distinctly and but once as far as reasonable. Avoid copying lists of words from the board. The single lessons can be mimeographed by the spelling teacher and a copy daily supplied to each child. If pasted in a penny blank book, they can be preserved by the child. The teacher should be close and accurate in correcting the writing spellers. Mistakes should not be overlooked.

Singing.

A few choice patriotic songs, hymns, and pleasing selections of a lighter character should be learned by heart each term by all the children of this grade. There should be some preliminary drill before the whole school in the thought and oral rendering of the verses, before they are set to music. The music itself, before the words are applied to it, may furnish good exercises in singing notes and simple measures.

For the Third Grade.

The songs and tunes selected should be the choicest and best.

Songs for Third Grade.

This is the Way the Snow Comes Down. (Dainty Songs.)

Beautiful Rain. (Dainty Songs.)

A Little Thing Like That. (Dainty Songs.)

The Clock. (Dainty Songs.)

Robin Redbreast. Leslie's Fountain Song book, published by A. Flanagan, Chicago.

America.

A Queer Little House. (Child's Song Book.)

The Fairy Artist. (Child's Song Book.)

Come Little Leaves. (Child's Song Book.)

Swing, Cradle, Swing. (Child's Song Book.)

Little Miss Snowflake. (Child's Song Book.)

See the Model Music Course, first and second readers.

Fourth Grade.

Each teacher in the fourth grade should make a study of the entire work of the grade. In this grade, perhaps, better than any other, can be seen those relations of studies to one another which the theory of concentration requires. The history stories, geography, science, and language are easily brought into many close and natural relations. The drawing is probably capable of rendering great service to the other studies in this grade. It will be interesting even in arithmetic to see how far the other studies furnish good concrete examples of reckoning such as are needed in this year. It will be well also to keep in mind the geography, literature, reading, and science studies of the preceding year. Keep the children individually and collectively in mind, and judge the fitness of the materials of study to their temper and capacity.

Reading.

The materials for reading in the fourth grade are drawn chiefly from the field of classic myth, both prose and verse. In the oral lessons of third grade the children have learned to appreciate some of the myths. The teacher should make a study of the chief books of myths, as indicated in the Special Method in Reading. There is great variety in this material. It gives the teacher a chance to make a closer acquaintance with a good portion of the most classic and famous literature of the world. If it leads the teacher to a reading of Bryant's or Pope's translations of Homer or Virgil, or Spencer's poems, the time will be well spent. Look in the library for the larger editions and illustrations of the works of these great poets. Use the geographies when needed.

First Term. Fall.

1. Kingsley's Greek Heroes.
2. Six Stories from the Arabian Nights.

As an alternate book for Greek Heroes use Hawthorne's Wonder Book.

3. Select poems from Open Sesame Vol. I.

The story of the Odyssey (Macmillan) may serve for sight reading and home reading by the children.

Children should be led first into the thought and spirit of the author, but thorough drills should follow. Use phonic and concert drill. The recitation of poems or selections committed to memory, singly and in concert, should daily occupy a small amount of time. Children can not be expected to buy more than one book during the term. The others should be supplied by the school.

Second Term. Winter.

4. Ulysses Among the Phaeacians.
5. Kingsley's Water Babies, or Hawthorne's Tanglewood Tales.
6. For sight reading, Tales from Spencer.
7. For memory selections, use Open Sesame, Vols. 1 and 2.

Stories from the History of Rome are good sight and home reading. Study the Special Method in Reading for suggestion. Notice what the children like, and what they work at with most spirit. Notice what books they are inclined to read at home and at their leisure. Put books in their way so as to test them and discover how far the taste for good books can be cultivated at this age. It may be well to call their attention to those books in the library which you think likely to suit them, and then observe what effect it has.

Third Term. Spring.

8. Heroes of Asgard.
9. For sight reading, Homer's Iliad.
10. Later, read Homer's Iliad, Book 1-8.
11. For sight reading use also Gods and Heroes, and Gulliver's Travels.
12. Open Sesame and Ballad Book for selections.

Selections appropriate to the season and to Arbor day and Decoration day should be found by the teacher and used. The history stories used in the oral work of this year may suggest also some story books for outside reading. The science and geography lessons may also suggest some poems and selections not given in the readers. Do not be discouraged with a book because it is difficult at the start, if its thought is really suited to the children.

Arithmetic.

Notice the work laid down for third grade. A variety of reviews and tests on this work may be well made at the beginning of the year. Children gain strength and quickness in arithmetical work according as they fully master and use what they have already learned.

Interest and attention in arithmetic depend upon the vigor and variety of class-room work. Study Cook's Methods of Written Arithmetic for forms of explanation, correctness, and accuracy in language, variety of class exercises at the board and the correction of common faults and errors. Insist on neatness and care in board work and in papers handed in. Keep the whole class busy with profitable work: do not allow one child to absorb the attention of the teacher to the neglect of the class. In assigning lessons be careful, moderate, regular, and definite.

For the Fourth Grade.

First Term. Fall.

Multiplication tables of 11's and 12's.

Oral drills, (a) rapid addition, subtraction, etc., designed to review previous work and give perfect mastery of the simple facts of arithmetic; (b) simple illustrative problems involving the same principles as the written work, and serving as an introduction to the written work.

Solution of problems involving the use of fractions as $\frac{1}{8}$ of 72, $\frac{2}{3}$ of 30, $\frac{1}{2}$ of 40, etc. Add and subtract three, four, and five place numbers. Multiply four, five, and six place numbers by two, three, and four place multiplier.

Short division—dividend a six place number. Review long measure, study and apply square measure. Study the areas of rectangles, fields, etc. Make simple reductions. Text, Cook and Cropsey, to p. 173.

Second Term. Winter.

Arabic notation and numeration through nine orders. Picture the numbers distinctly before writing. Give great variety of oral exercises, and do not use pencil or crayon when children can do the work without such aid. Children often work mechanically when it is much better for them simply to think the operations.

Review long measure and square measure, illustrate and apply cubic measure. Much practice in subtraction and multiplication for speed and accuracy. Review short division with divisor up to 12. Long division. Show the relation between long division and short division. Notice the concrete problems naturally suggested by other studies. With objects and diagrams illustrate simple fractions. Apply by getting the fractional parts of numbers mentally. Cook and Cropsey to 199.

Third Term. Spring.

Continue practice in long division. Study objectively and apply by measurements, dry measure, liquid measure, avoirdupois weight, and time measure. Work simple examples in reduction ascending and descending.

Oral and written problems involving the four fundamental operations and compound numbers should alternate. Continue exercises in simple fractions. Let the exercises be vigorous thought work rather than mechanical. Cook and Cropsey, 199-230.

Geography.

The year's work includes twenty important topics on the Mississippi Valley.

The general movement is from the home state outwards, and is synthetic. But we must use frequently the map of the United States, of North America, and of the world. Study maps and make maps, and realize the facts of surface and the proportion of parts. The broader survey and comparison at the close of important topics will give chance for forming large groups and districts based on a common character, as the forest regions, arid regions, etc. Use pictures and diagrams to make clear and objective the ideas presented. The presentation by the teacher should be chiefly oral, with questions discussed, systematic presentation and reproduction in full, clear, and definite form. Keep outlines of topics treated and record regularly in the outline book. Every important geographical type should be clearly grasped by the teacher in its central idea and presented from that standpoint. The important relations to other studies, as science or history, should be noticed, but should not lead astray. Notice especially the relations to history, natural science, and literature. The drawing may also greatly aid the geography. Be careful and persistent in the use of good English in oral and written work. In geography the teacher must exercise a strong and clear imagination that projects definite pictures. The children must develop a like ability. Use home material and experience as illustrative. Notice the work of third grade and its scope.

Study the method as well as the material in Special Method in Geography.

In geography the children recite every other day.

First Term. Fall.

Treat the following type studies fully:

The Illinois River, The prairies of Illinois, the corn and live stock in Illinois, the coal mines of Illinois: a trip on the Upper Mississippi, lumbering in Minnesota. Minneapolis as a trade center.

Incidental to these topics will come the chief cities and surface of Illinois, the study of its surface and map, its commerce and people.

In connection with the Upper Mississippi and Minneapolis is a clear grasp of the great productive regions of the Northwest. The wheat region, the pineries, the railroads, cities, etc. Certain great trade routes leading to Chicago may also be indicated and the reason for them seen. States are located and drawn, cities studied, and climatic and surface features made very clear.

Second Term. Winter.

Important type studies as follows: Lake Superior (compared with Lake Michigan). The iron mines of Michigan (the blast furnace). The hard-wood forests of Indiana (Ohio valley). Chicago as a trade center (the lake ports). Tobacco raising in Kentucky (tobacco region). The surface of Tennessee. The Lower Mississippi.

It is possible to form important series of cities and trade routes in this term's work. City should be compared with city, river with river, lake with lake, state with state; as Minneapolis with Pittsburg, etc. Contrasts are also important.

Use a large wall map and all illustrative materials, keeping before the children the broader relations of the whole country.

The knowledge and mastery of the children should be tested by written work as well as by oral reproductions. For material and suggestion consult the Special Method in Geography. Keep outlines of all work in the outline books.

Third Term. Spring.

Type studies as follows: Springfield and the state government of Illinois. Cotton raising in Mississippi (the cotton belt). Sugar in Louisana. The cattle ranch of Texas (the great grazing region of the plains). Pike's Peak and vicinity. Irrigation in Colorado. Yellowstone Park.

In finishing up the Mississippi valley at the end of this year's work we should make broader reviews and comparisons of all the great productive regions and objects in the broad valley. Compare and contrast the Ohio valley and the Missouri valley. Compare the pineries of the north with the hard-wood forests of the south; the arid region of the west with the moist, rainy regions farther east. Notice the cities and centers of population, and those regions but slightly settled; give reasons. Notice differences in climate and products, north and south, east and west, and the reasons. Dwell upon and master the facts.

History Stories.

In the fourth grade the children take up the pioneer history stories of the Mississippi Valley. They run largely parallel with the geographical topics of the year and yet, while closely related at every step, they are not made directly dependent one upon the other.

Much study of maps and geographical conditions will be necessary to understand the stories, and the stories lend a great interest to many parts of the country studied in the geography.

The history lessons come on alternate days and are mainly oral presentations by the teacher, clear and connected in their topics, graphic, using illustrative materials, diagrams, maps, and vivid descriptions. The work should be systematic and logical, ending in definite outlines of topics which the children insert in their outline book. By means of questions and discussion, the children should be made inquisitive, thoughtful, and self-active. Let them reproduce the stories in the main orally, with proper care as to correctness in language. A good story is one of the best means in the world for teaching children to use good English naturally. Let the corrections be quiet and persistent. As the class advances it can give some brief reproductions in writing. The children should feel and realize the hardships and difficulties and dangers which the early pioneers underwent. The strong qualities, the virtues, and personal traits, should be clearly seen and appreciated, as they furnish the deeper quality and value of such instruction. These stories should lead up to a respect and love for American history as a field of study very attractive and stimulating to the children themselves.

First Term. Fall.

Marquette and Joliet's voyage. LaSalle on the Lakes and in Illinois. Hennepin's voyage on the Upper Mississippi. George R. Clark at Kaskaskia and Vincennes.

No absolute order for these stories can be fixed. The chronological idea does not control their order. It is well to begin with stories of the home state. It may be well to precede these stories with some local facts and stories in the history of the town or neighborhood, and its first settlement. In narrating these stories it is well to use a map of the United States or of North America. Better still is a simple sketch drawn on the blackboard by the teacher and enlarged and extended little by little as the story proceeds. This brings out the details and places very clearly. Combine this plan with the use of wall maps. Let children sketch also.

Second Term. Winter.

Lincoln's early life.
The Sioux Massacre of 1862.
Boone as hunter and settler in Kentucky.
Robertson and the settlement of Tennessee.
Settlement of Marietta and Cincinnati.

These stories bring out moral ideas and character. Children should be allowed to express their judgment of men's acts in a natural way. Some acts they will condemn, as Kenton's, others they will admire and approve.

It is not necessary to moralize and make such discussions distasteful. Children have a moral sense and should be allowed to cultivate their moral judgments on such materials.

For a full discussion of the oral method of teaching such stories consult the Special Method in Literature and History, pp. 69-84.

Third Term. Spring.

LaSalle on the Lower Mississippi.
Lewis and Clarke on the Missouri.
Fremont on the Plains and in the Mountains.
DeSoto's discovery of the Mississippi.

As children become more accustomed to this kind of oral work, they should increase in power and capacity to receive and express such ideas. Cultivate thoughtfulness, reasoning, and self-activity in the discussions. Do not turn them into simple narratives and reproductions. Make everything real and graphic. Compare the men with each other in their journeys and hazardous enterprises.

Keep your eye to what is going on in the other studies, and see how the studies may be properly related. Adapt the instruction to individual children, and notice whether all children take an interest in such biographical stories.

Natural Science.

In selecting and treating the science topics of this year several things must be kept in mind.

1. The suggestions of the seasons.
2. The age and previous science knowledge of the pupils.
3. The suggestions of the other studies, especially history and geography.
4. The inter-relations between the science topics themselves, as important types or as forming a group of mutually dependent things in nature, such as the forest, pond, river, prairie, etc.

Two things should be kept in mind upon excursions and in all observations. Center attention upon a few important types whether animal, plant, mineral, etc. Keep the eyes open also for all objects of interest.

The children are old enough in this grade to begin to understand life-groups in nature and to trace the dependence of animal upon plant environment, etc.

The life histories should be kept up, *i. e.*, the complete biography of animal or plant, so that the work of the three terms may be in part continuous, noticing, *e. g.*, the fall, winter, and spring appearance and growth of a plant.

Language descriptions and drawings are only means of testing and aiding close observation. Notice the science work of the third grade and utilize it. Do not confine the science work to the topics outlined if others more important and suitable are suggested. Observe the close relations of the science topics to the other studies.

First Term. Fall.

1. *Forests.*—Hickory, walnut, birch, oak, grape vine (wild and cultivated), plum (wild and cultivated), chestnut. sumac.
2. *Rivers* and *ponds.*—Catfish, turtle, clam, frog, beaver, otter, wild rice, cranberry.
3. *Prairie* and *Field.*—Buffalo, turkey (wild and tame), prairie chicken, ox-eye daisy, goldenrod, wild grass, ground squirrel, prairie dog.
4. *Mineral.*—Coal and its formation, limestone, and other strata.
5. *Atmosphere.*—Ventilation, explosives, safety lamp. Varieties of weather, wind and temperature.

Second Term. Winter.

Continue topics of previous term.

1. *Forests.*—Evergreen forests in winter. Deer, moose, ox (stomach).
2. *Rivers.*—Fish, turtles, frogs, in winter. Sources of rivers, springs, wells, pumps.
3. *Minerals.*—Rock strata, clay, copper, gold, mineral springs.
4. *Atmosphere.*—Thermometer, observations and records. Evaporation, rain, snow, direction of winds.
5. *Sun.*—Sun light, sun glass, prism, colors. Position of sun.
6.—*Indian Antiquities.*—Relics, arrow heads, mounds, food, clothing, tents, weapons for hunting and war.

Third Term. Spring.

Continue topics begun in the fall and winter.

1. *Forests.*—Cottonwood, birch, sycamore, locust, plum, grape, cherry. Bloodroot, hepatica. Varieties of woodpecker, turtle dove, tanager.
2. *Swamp.*—Marsh marigold, crayfish, willow, soil of marshes.

3. *Meadow.*—Tame and wild grasses, dock, lark, thrush, bob-white.

4. *Sun*—Its changes of position. The moon and its phases.

5. *The Atmosphere.*—The barometer. Frost, clouds, dew, hail.

6. *Indian Antiquities.*—Baskets and house implements, boats.

Language Lessons.

Read the plan for language in third grade. The lessons are upon alternate days, and are planned to teach the correct use of good English, both oral and written. The aim of the lessons is not to teach grammar nor the rules of grammar. The composition exercises, which call for two lessons out of five, are derived largely from the outlines previously worked over in geography, history, etc. The oral exercises in language are given up to the drills upon correct forms of speech in which errors are commonly made. The lessons in history, geography, and natural science give, incidentally, sufficient drill in descriptive and narrative English. Special drill in language lessons of this sort are not needed, if teachers are careful to correct errors in speech occurring in those studies. Language teachers should acquaint themselves with what is going on in the other fourth grade studies, so as to use their materials in language exercises.

First Term. Fall.

Use Bright's Outline for Fourth Grade. Review and apply the work of previous grades.

For suggestive exercises use DeGarmo's No. II., parts 3 and 4.

Give variety of composition exercises, letters, dictations, quotations, with outline and without outline. Observe punctuation, abbreviations, capitals, paragraphing, spelling, and correct grammatical forms.

Introduce children to the use of the dictionary.

Record in the outline books under language lessons, the classes of words studied, as, irregular verbs, homonyms, pronouns, etc., and any principles and rules of work developed by the instruction.

Second Term. Winter.

Continue the work of previous term. Preserve the compositions so as to mark the progress of pupils. All compositions written the second time should be in the outline book.

In the use of the dictionary study the diacritical markings and make their use familiar. In oral language use thought materials worthy of attention.

In the reading and other studies find illustrations of the same usages required in the language lessons. The home and play-ground language of the children should be drawn upon and criticised or used for illustration.

Third Term. Spring.

Complete Bright's fourth grade work. Use De Garmo's No. III. for suggestive exercises. Give variety of drills in dictation, board exercises, and compositions.

When children write exercises in the class let the teacher guard against faults by preliminary suggestions. Let pointed board exercises correct faults in composition. Insist upon carefulness and neatness. Do not accept careless and slovenly papers. Use the vertical writing in compositions and consult with the writing teacher.

Drawing.

In this grade drawing is still mainly tributary to the other studies. Consult Miss Gertrude A. Stoker's "Seeing and Doing," especially fourth grade work. Read also her introduction to drawing. The teacher in drawing will need to examine the work going on in other classes of this grade so as to select appropriate drawing topics. The drawings of each child should be preserved both as an encouragement to the pupil and as illustrative of other lessons. Encourage freedom of movement but insist on neatness and carefulness. The drawing work is done in the presence of the teacher. She should guard against palpable errors,

The work for each term is well suggested in Miss Stoker's outline, but many other similar and appropriate objects may be suggested by the season or by other studies. Some topics suggested by history are as follows: Tents, forts, boats, trees, guns, animals, etc.; by the geography, are coal mines, rock strata, bridges, houses (lumber camp), cañons, machines, docks, mountains, etc.; by the natural science, are seedling plants, flowers, insects, fishes, deer, rabbit, etc. Consult the remarks and plans for drawing in third grade.

Spelling.

The spelling exercises of fourth grade are carried on according to the same plan as that of third grade. The words are selected by teachers in the different studies and deposited weekly with the room-teacher, to be used for written spelling lessons by the spelling teacher. The application of good spelling is necessary in all classes, as in reading, geography, language lessons, natural science, and composition or written work. Encourage also the reference to the dictionary for spelling as well as for pronunciations. Examine carefully the plan for spelling in third grade.

Writing.

Study the plan of work in writing outlined in third grade. Continue the drill exercises there begun. Notice the effect of the writing exercises upon the usual written exercises outside of the writing period.

The list of science books suggested for third and fifth grades should be examined by the teachers.

Let the children memorize the words of a number of classic songs and learn to sing them well. Use the Model Music Course first and second readers.

Use also the songs learned in third grade.

Consult also the remarks on music in third grade.

Fifth Grade.

In this grade we take the pioneer biographies of the eastern states and of the ocean explorers and parallel with this the geography of the Atlantic states, of the United States as a whole, and of North America. The classic readings of this grade are selected partly from American and partly from European authors and subjects. Some of the best longer and shorter classics, both prose and verse, should be read in the regular reading exercises of this grade. Many of the science topics will be suggested by the history, geography, and literature of this grade. The language lessons and drawing will also stand in close dependence upon the other studies.

Much of the work in history, language, geography, and natural science is oral and it should be made systematic and effective. Throw the children constantly upon their own resources. Hold them responsible for thoughtfulness, inventiveness, self-activity, and a clear and full reproduction, either orally or in writing, of topics discussed. Give them thought material worthy of their interest and effort and hold them to its mastery. They are inclined to be careless in all formal exercises. In a good-tempered but persistent way accept only careful and neat work. Simply marking down to 60 or 70 will not cure them of careless habits and poor work. In the class room they should be held to great attentiveness, diligence, and genuine mastery of their tasks, but do not expect much outside study. If boys and girls at this age can be encouraged to read some of the best books suggested in the collateral reading courses it will do them great good. Excellent books in biography, science, and literature can be recommended to them. The room teacher may do well to keep track of what the children are selecting from the library for leisure hour reading. Some suggestions along this line for the whole school may be wholesome for the children. Consult the lists in Special Method in Reading.

Reading.
First Term. Fall.

Whittier's Barefoot Boy.

Hiawatha. Part I. Part II, Home reading.

Black Beauty. Part in class and part for home reading.

Difficulties are apt to meet the teacher in the first lessons upon a longer classic. The style and language are unusual and therefore difficult. For sight reading in class and for home reading, recommend some of the fourth grade books not yet read, as Gulliver's Travels or Tales of Spenser. Also Tales from English History.

For memorizing select poems from Children's Treasury of English Song, and the Ballad Book.

Second Term. Winter.

King of the Golden River.

Sohrab and Rustum (may be too hard).

Read parts of Higginson's American Explorers. Select poems and stories from Songs of Labor, Children's Treasury of English Songs, and Book of Golden Deeds. For home and sight reading use Stories of Our Country, Stories of Herodotus, and others. Find out what excellent things children like to read for themselves, and what they can learn to like. For method, consult Special Method in Reading. Get acquainted with the literature of this grade. Study the temper and character of particular children as influenced or not by literature.

For the Fifth Grade. 71

Third Term. Spring.

Lays of Ancient Rome.

Continue Higginson's American Explorers. Select choice poems for memorizing. Tales of Chivalry for sight reading. Outside reading. Ten Boys on the Road from Long Ago. Book of Golden Deeds. Wake Robin, etc.

In this grade we may well test children as to their capacity and readiness to appreciate biographical history and choice literature. It is well to work with the parents in selecting and encouraging the reading of appropriate books. Some children read too much and in a slipshod way. More children should read choice books.

History.

The history of this year consists of biographical stories of the pioneer explorers along the Atlantic sea board, also the stories of the great ocean pioneers, and of California and the extreme west. The lessons are treated, in the main, orally, with thorough reproductions, oral or written, by the children. All the devices for graphic presentation should be used, diagrams, maps. board sketches, pictures and descriptive detail of persons, events and places. The work should be instructive, interesting and strong in the presentation of manly characters, meeting difficulties and hardships bravely and steadily. This awakens strong interests in those parts of American history which children can appreciate. A good deal of the geography of America and of Europe are necessary to the understanding of the stories. It will be found that the geography of the year helps greatly the comprehension of the stories. The language drill in good oral speech, furnished by the stories, is of the best quality. Correct errors in language and insist on full and original language expression. Study carefully the chapter on Pioneer History Stories in the Special Method in Literature and History. Let each child keep the full outline of topics in his outline book, neatly written in ink. As far as time permits, read Parkman, Roosevelt and other historians for fuller accounts of these men and events.

First Term. Fall.

Champlain and his expeditions.
Hudson and his trip up the river.
John Smith in Virginia.
Sir Walter Raleigh and his attempts.

These stories are not based on chronology as a leading idea. They are simply attempts to bring out the life and character of great pioneer leaders who opened up a large new world. They are biographical pictures and should be made as real and life-like as possible. Interesting comparisons of the men with each other may fittingly close the stories. Some of the children may begin to read collateral books as suggested by the stories.

Second Term. Winter.

The story of Columbus and the discovery. Magellan and the first trip around the world. Cortes and the conquest of Mexico. These stories take in the world whole. Europe, the Atlantic, America, the Pacific, the Italian and the Spaniard, as well as the Frenchman and the Englishman, are revealed in their character. Provide for a proper setting of the stories in the geography. Very interesting comparisons of leading characters are possible. In these detailed biographical stories there is a fine preparation for an understanding of later history and geography. The native races are also seen in an interesting light.

Third Term. Spring.

The Story of the Pilgrims at Plymouth.
The Early Life of Washington to Braddock's Defeat.
Fremont Crossing the Sierra Nevada to California.

Trip Across the Plains and Mountains to California in 1849.

These stories bring us back to our own country more closely, and to its earlier and later pioneer difficulties.

Notice the course in geography for fifth grade, and see its relation to the history. Keep the two separate, but trace their relations. The work in all these stories centers in the biographical interest. Notice the history of fourth grade. Study the other work of the fifth grade.

Geography.

The lessons of this grade (fifth) include about thirty important type studies, taken from the Atlantic slope, the Pacific slope, Canada and Mexico, and North America as a whole. In the geography, as well as in the history of this year, it will be necessary to use at times the maps and globes showing the earth-whole. The topics will still be presented mainly in oral form by the teacher, and discussed and reproduced by the pupil. Systematic outlines will be kept. Children should sketch maps on the board and on paper. Surface features should be made in sand. Frye's Geography will be helpful. Study the plan and method of the Special Method in Geography. Every important type study should not only be presented in its descriptive and instructive detail, but sufficient additional objects of the same kind should be examined and compared with the type to show the scope of the idea on a large scale in the geography of North America. Great commercial routes and centers of traffic should be seen in their importance. Series of causally related objects should be linked together and the common cause noted. The lesser facts of geography should be seen in their proper relation to the more important ones. To some extent children can read collateral information books, such as geographical readers, and report upon the topics in class.

First Term. Fall.

Hudson River. Adirondacks, and Erie Canal.

Mt. Washington. (White Mountains. Scenery. Summer resorts).

Boston (history, monuments, commerce, institutions).

A Cotton-Mill at Lowell. (Merrimac water power. Manufactures of New England. Shipping cotton and cloth).

Ship-Building at Philadelphia. (Ship-yards. Navy-yards).

Washington. (Government. Compare with state government).

The Oyster Fisheries of the Chesapeake. (Long Island Sound).

The James River and Surface Features of Virginia. Richmond.

The Pineries of Carolina. (Ships' supplies, ports).

Orange Groves in Florida. (Resorts, climate).

The old type studies of the Mississippi valley will suggest valuable comparisons with the topics of the Atlantic slope. Besides this, important extensions of those old topics into the Eastern states should be noticed, *e.g.*, the pine forests and lumbering of Maine, etc.

Second Term. Winter.

New York City as a trade center.

The Central Pacific Railroad. (Compare).

A gold mine in California. (Gold area).

The Colorado River. Cañons.

The Salt Lake Basin. (Humboldt River).

Salmon Fisheries of the Columbia.

San Francisco. (Compare with New York).

Trip from Puget Sound to Alaska.

The previous studies in geography furnish many points of comparison and many opportunities to extend and apply types previously studied, *e. g.*, irrigation, coal mines, mountains, fruit growing, climate, etc. Children should do some reference study. Lessons mainly oral. Use and make maps.

Third Term. Spring.

The St. Lawrence River. (Scenery, cities).
Cod-fishing on the banks. (Compare).
The City of Mexico. (Plateau, climate).
Popocatepetl. (Mt. Ranier, St. Elias, etc).
A banana farm in Jamaica. (Islands).
The Rocky Mountains as a whole.
The River systems and slopes of North America.
The commercial routes of North America.
The continent of North America as a whole.

Every topic studied should become the center and rallying point for a large body of closely associated ideas. Notice the close connections with other studies, but do not allow these connections to mislead into confusion of ideas and studies.

Natural Science.

These lessons come every other day, are essentially oral, should be systematic, with keeping of careful outlines. The life groups partly developed in fourth grade should be still further developed and extended in fifth grade.

The larger notion of zones, with the idea of characteristic plant, animal and climate in each may be much helped by the science lessons. Teachers as well as pupils need to cultivate a close observation of the objects and phenomena of science about home, also to use the best monographs in science to help them in their studies. The biographies of some of the famous scientists may be consulted and drawn upon to lend interest to some of the studies of this year. Hugh Miller, for example, in geology, Agassiz in the study of fishes, Gray in connection with the study of plants, etc.

Keep posted on the science topics previously studied by the children. Extend and strengthen the groups already studied. An examination of the adaptation of the plant (cactus) or animal (fish) to its environment, the fitness of organs and structure to the mode of life suggest deep and interesting thoughts to the children. Let children learn to respect and love things in nature, to see the beauty and wonders in nature but not to be destructive or give pain or lay waste and spoil.

First Term. Fall.

Insect life. The bee, a hive of bees, queen bee, etc. (Compare with bumble bee, wasp.)

Migrations of Birds. Black bird, rice bird.

Forests are studied incidental to the topics above.

Animal life in water. (Clam,) oyster, cod-fish, salmon, (seal), whale, polar bear.

Recall the study of river fish in fourth grade.

Fruits. The peach (other stone fruit), the orange, lemon, banana, cocoanut.

The steam engine. Expansion by heat. Applications to commerce and manufacturing.

Make a full, detailed study of at least one object and its life history in each of the five topics. Then compare and extend the idea. Get the facts from observations, from books, from specialists. Trace connections with other studies.

Second Term. Winter.

Light and the Eye. The eye of an ox, parts and functions. The human eye. Light, reflection and refraction, mirrors, lenses, telescope, and microscope.

Minerals. The crust of the earth, geologic strata, pebbles, boulders, limestone, granite, marble, the gravel bank, quartz, the gorge and erosion, glaciers, volcanoes fossils, geological history.

The moon and its phases. The tides.
The compass, the magnet.
In most cases the objects for study can be brought into the school-room; collections of rocks and minerals can be made by the children for the school room. Let the class-room descriptions and discussions be based upon the previous observations and collections of the children.

Third Term. Spring.

Migration of Birds in spring time. The water birds.
Continue the study of *rock strata*, mineral ores, mountain building, springs, artesian wells.
Plants. Pitch pine, cactus, California red-wood, ebony, rosewood, palm tree, ferns, mosses, tobacco plants.
Salt. Mines, springs, lakes.
The *milk weed butterfly.* Egg, life, changes, food, movements, structure, migration.
Movements of the earth about the sun.
Consult the Special Method for natural science. Study the work of the whole year and keep up the study of topics begun earlier in the year. Test the children by oral work, writing, and drawing.

Science Books for Fifth Grade.

Winchell's Geological Excursions.
The Beauties of Nature (Lubbock), Macmillan.
The Life of a Butterfly (Scudder), Henry Holt & Co., New York City.
Birds and Bees (Burroughs), Houghton, Mifflin & Co.
Up and Down the Brooks, Houghton, Mifflin & Co.
Ants, Bees, and Wasps (Lubbock), D. Appleton & Co., New York.
Among the Trees, Mrs. Dyson.
Wake Robin (Burroughs), Houghton, Mifflin & Co.
Coal and Coal Mines, Houghton, Mifflin & Co.
Madam How and Lady Why (Kingsley), Macmillan.

Seaside and Wayside, No. III and No. IV., D. C. Heath & Co.

Animal Memoirs, Part I, Mammals; Part II, Birds, Iveson, Blakeman & Co., Chicago.

Directions for Teaching Geology (pamphlet) (Shaler), D. C. Heath & Co.

First Book in Geology (Shaler), D. C. Heath & Co.

The Great World's Farm (Gaye), Seeley & Co.

Language Lessons.

As in third and fourth grades the lessons are divided between oral drills upon correct forms and composition exercises. Read closely the plan outlined for third grade. Freedom and accuracy in the use of common English (both oral and written) are the aims of the lesson. Do not accept careless written work. Give variety of lively drills, oral, on black-board, dictations, compositions on given outlines, compositions without outlines, the use in sentences of irregular forms, abbreviations, contractions and quotations. Write up excursions, geographical and scientific. Write about books the children have read. Observe the children in the midst of the composition work and guard against errors.

First Term. Fall.

Begin Bright's outline for fifth grade. Review the work of third and fourth grades and apply the facts there learned.

Begin DeGarmo No. III. These lessons are suggestive rather than illustrative.

The composition exercises of fifth grade should show independence and individuality and capacity for expression. The papers should be longer and fuller than in earlier grades. Preserve the compositions. Put some of them in the letter form.

Continue from fourth grade work in the use of the dictionary. Learn to use and interpret by the diacritical markings. Put the language lessons, both oral and written, into close relation with other studies.

Second Term. Winter.

Continue Bright's fifth grade work.
Continue DeGarmo's Part III.
Continue the dictionary work.
Examine the literature the children have been studying for illustrations and tests of what the children have learned in language lessons. Bring in a variety of letters, business and friendly, to test the rules developed. Dramatic and dialogue selections will furnish good tests of punctuation, capitals, contractions, and correct forms of expression. Use technical grammatical terms when needed, but give simple explanations of their meaning, without special care as to their strict grammatical definitions. Use rules only when they help correct speech.

Third Term. Spring.

Complete Bright's fifth grade work.
Use DeGarmo's Part III.
Be sure the children know how to use the dictionary. Teach them also the use of cyclopedia, atlas, and other reference books.
Continue to use the literature previously studied as a basis of illustrating and testing the forms of English.
Write out quotations from memory. Write stories from memory. Write on the lives of certain authors studied. Write upon excursions, holidays, vacations, etc. Apply the language facts learned to other studies, to life, to home conversations, to newspapers. Collect errors from all sources, and discuss in the class.

Arithmetic.

Study the preface to the arithmetic, and examine the book as a whole to get its plan, purpose, and method.

Study Cook's Methods in Written Arithmetic to see correct forms of explanation, to avoid common errors in arithmetical language, to make the work thought exercises instead of formal mechanical drills. Work all examples mentally which can be reasonably done so. Use abundance of oral drills for the sake of review, for rapid use of old facts, and for the introduction and explanation of new principles. Let both teacher and pupils illustrate problems with objects and with board diagrams. Let children test and prove their own results, not depending on the book, teacher, or anybody else. Let the children see how to use old ideas and principles in new cases and problems. Trace up closely the relations between the different parts of arithmetic.

The other studies will furnish many problems that can be worked out by the pupils, *e.g*, the areas of belts or regions of production, as the hard wood forests, prairies, river valleys, the quantity of products, etc. The natural science and history stories also furnish problems.

Examine closely the plan of arithmetic in third and fourth grades.

First Term. Fall.

Text-book, Cook and Cropsey, begin p. 230. Simple fractions.

Illustrate objectively and cause the children to illustrate and invent illustrations. Introduce simple oral problems in approaching any principle or rule. Get the rule inductively by comparing illustrative problems. Make a rule, compare it with the one in the book. Apply it to a variety of particular cases. Besides the book problems, make others from familiar objects and from other studies. Precision in language should follow clear perception of relations. Think out the problem in its essentials before beginning to figure it out.

Second Term. Winter.

Cook and Cropsey.

Continue the study of fractions, simple and decimal. Learn to handle the class at the board. Keep all busy at profitable work. Let board work be neat and careful. The drill exercises should be energetic and rapid with breathing spaces between the problems.

If papers are called for with home work they should be forthcoming and not overlooked or neglected. Do not assign too much home work. Do not stop to help backward pupils at the expense of the whole class. Assign lessons carefully, reasonably, considering the ability of the pupils.

Third Term. Spring.

Cook and Cropsey.

Finish common and decimal fractions. Do not seek to work complex and difficult problems so much as to master the simple principles and apply them rapidly to a great variety of simple material.

Oral drills involving all the previous facts and operations of arithmetic should be frequent. Put variety of work into each recitation. Study closely the plans for the whole year's work.

Avoid slow and mechanical habits. Make the thought work prominent. Apply the formal steps to arithmetic work. Self reliance and vigor are the results much desired in pupils.

Drawing.

The drawing of fifth grade is largely dependent upon the objects suggested by the other studies.

For the general plan, consult Miss Stoker's "Seeing and Doing." Notice the general plan of the book and the special work of fifth grade.

The science topics in this grade will furnish many objects for molding, cutting, and drawing, *e.g.*, fruits, trees, geologic strata, birds, instruments, etc.; the history suggests buildings, temples, log-houses and forts, ships, tropical trees, etc.; the geography suggests canal boats, mills, public buildings, cañons, bluffs, islands, mountains, and volcanoes.

Writing.

The writing should be a careful drill in the vertical script.

Consult closely Mr. Cavins' plan as outlined for third grade.

Children of this age, especially boys, are apt to be careless in writing. Insist upon care in position, neatness, and obedience to requirements. Apply the same method of vertical writing to all the written exercises of the class. See whether other teachers of this grade are applying these requirements in written exercises, *e.g.*, spelling, compositions, and board work. Make the writing exercises superfluous as soon as possible. Excuse from it those who have attained proficiency and have established good habits.

Music.

Children in this grade should memorize the words and music of a number of classic songs.

1. Patriotic songs, familiar and popular.
2. Songs fitted to the seasons and age of the children.
3. Hymns (both words and music classic).
4. Songs suggested by the nature studies.

In connection with these songs it is possible to bring in certain drills which will give children a mastery of the elements of music. Teachers should make a special effort to make the acquaintance of these songs and learn how to use them in schools. For songs, consult the Model Music Course for Schools. Third Reader.

Spelling.

The spelling lessons are drawn from the other studies. Lists of words are made each week by each teacher and left on file with the room-teacher to be used for the spelling class.

Consult the plan fully outlined in third grade. Use Sherwood's Writing Speller. Get neat written work. Use pen, ink, and blotter. Correct words carefully. Drill on corrected words. Notice the meaning of words.

Sixth Grade.

The work of the studies in sixth grade consists of a body of closely related materials from literature, history, natural science, geography, and language. Each teacher in this grade should examine the whole course for the year, and, as far as time permits, make a closer acquaintance with the material of the different studies. There is a certain unity which binds them all together and makes them dependent upon one another. On the principle of concentration the topics in the different studies are selected along parallel lines. The history stories of the fifth grade and the colonial history of the sixth grade are closely associated with the literature of the colonial period used as reading matter in the sixth grade. The geography of Europe is intimately linked with the stories of the pioneer explorers in the fifth grade, with the colononial history, and with the literature of Scotland, England, and other countries of Europe used as reading matter in sixth grade, and even earlier. The science lessons at many points touch the geography and history of the same grade closely. The language and composition work should be brought into touch with the most interesting topics in literature, geography, and natural science, so as to make it more real and less formal. Keep in mind always the fitness of the material for the children.

Reading.
First Term. Fall.

Grandfather's Chair (Hawthorne), Houghton, Mifflin & Co. Select the best stories—do not try to read the book entire. The Sketch Book, Rip Van Winkle, and Sleepy Hollow. Selected poems from the Golden Treasury of Songs and Lyrics. Memorize some of these, partly for individual and partly for concert recitation at the beginning of recitations. For sight reading and for collateral home reading, use Jason's Quest, The Stories of Waverly, and Bunyan's Pilgrim's Progress. For suggestions as to the spirit and method of the work, read chapters I, III, IV, and VI, of the Special Method in Reading. Let the teacher get acquainted with as much as she can of the literature suggested for this grade. The teacher should read and master a story or poem as a whole before trying to handle it with a class.

Second Term. Winter.

The Courtship of Miles Standish (Houghton, Mifflin & Co). The Autobiography of Benjamin Franklin (Houghton, Mifflin & Co., also Ginn & Co). The Lay of the Last Minstrel (Ginn & Co).

The Autobiography can be read only in part in the class but may be completed outside. For collateral reading, take Ten Great Events in History (Am. Book Co.), and Ivanhoe (Ginn & Co). Short poems should also be selected, and, after proper discussion and drill, memorized by the class.

Third Term. Spring.

Snow Bound and Among the Hills. Houghton, Mifflin & Co.

Birds and Bees. Houghton, Mifflin & Co.

Tales of a Grandfather (Scott). Ginn & Co.

The latter book cannot be read complete in the class, but some of its best parts should be read in a spirited way and enough interest awakened to lead to further reading. The Hunting of the Deer and the Christmas Carol may furnish good sight and collateral reading. The poems selected for memorizing should be in harmony with the other literature of the year. They should be selected at times to suit the season or the day celebrated.

The reading matter of this year is closely related in many ways to the previous reading, to the history and geography and natural science studied in earlier terms. Note these relations.

Sixth grade pupils may well read into the lines of the authors they are studying. The library should be used for this purpose. Much of the reference work however should be voluntary.

History.

The sixth grade history includes the period of colonial settlement and growth up to the beginning of the Revolution. The fourth and fifth grade pioneer stories have prepared the way for this history. The plan is to select four or five of the chief colonies as types and make a somewhat full study of a few leading topics in each colony. By omitting a greater part of what is usually learned as history we gain time for a deeper and more graphic account of a few very significant topics. The history will come on alternate days and should be partly oral, facts being presented by the teacher, and partly derived from books which the children read and report upon. In any case children should discuss and reason at the causes. The effort to grasp an important topic in a variety of relations gives good development to self activity and judgment. History should bring out with great force and clearness a few fundamental truths. The biographies of prominent colonial characters constitute a good share of the best material for this grade.

First Term. Fall.

Massachusetts as the typical New England colony. Sift out the important topics for full and careful study. A briefer reference to Connecticut and other New England colonies for the sake of comparison with Massachusetts. The development of government, town meeting, representative bodies, legislatures, governors, etc., needs close study.

The Pequot and King Philip's wars should be studied in detail.

The History of *Virginia* before the Revolution. Here also a few important topics should be handled fully. A comparison of people, government, and manner of life with Massachusetts will be fruitful.

The relations to the mother country in both colonies needs careful attention.

Second Term. Winter.

History of New York and the Iroquois. A somewhat full account of this great Indian confederacy should be aimed at. The History of Pennsylvania. As a collateral topic take the early history of Maryland. Use good biographies of such men as Wm. Penn, Stuyvesant, Benjamin Franklin, and others for reference work. Study the maps and physical features of the different colonies. The geography and parallel history of European countries are important in connection with the history of the colonies. The history will open the way for a better use of some of our best American classics, as, Courtship of Miles Standish, Sketch Book, Knickerbocker History, and, later, Evangeline.

Third Term. Spring.

The History of Georgia.
The efforts at colonial union.
The last French and Indian War.

The previous history has led up to an appreciation of the last great struggle between the French and English for the possession of North America. The biographies of Pitt, Washington, Wolf, Montcalm, and others will be used for reference. A full mastery of a few leading events and a sympathetic acquaintnce with the great characters of this epoch are better than a multitude of facts.

Geography.

Sixth grade geography is devoted mainly to Europe.

The plan of type studies will be continued through this grade. Each type study will require, on the average, two or three recitations. The topics are all new to the children and should, therefore, call out greater interest. In those important topics already fully treated in America only brief comparisons will be necessary, e. g., the coal mines and coal fields, the forests, grains, and live stock of Europe. The original standards with which we measure the government, industries, mountains, rivers, commerce, etc., of Europe are those already described fully in America. When the resemblance is very marked and not many new facts are to be brought out in Europe, a brief comparison with American topics is all that is necessary. The historical references in previous history stories, in the poems and myths of Europe should be referred to and made use of to help the geography. Study the plan and method of procedure in Special Method in Geography for fourth grade.

First Term. Fall.

Trip by steamer from New York to Liverpool. (A steamship line, commerce).

Home and estate of an English country gentleman. (Agriculture, landed gentry, tenants, parks).

Manchester as a manufacturing center. The raw materials, whence obtained, the ship canal; compare and locate other centers of manufacture.

Ship building at Glasgow. (Iron ships, war ships).

The Thames and shipping at London. Commerce of England.

The Parliament House, Windsor Castle, and the Tower. (The government of England; compare with the United States).

Westminster in London. (St. Paul's).

Oxford and Cambridge. (Compare with Harvard, etc).

The French people. (Language, history, character).

Paris, the city of arts. (Palaces, churches, streets, bridges, museums, parks, history, and monuments).

Around each of these important types we may collect a large body of similar facts, as we move on to the other countries of Europe and as we call up types previously studied. For example, Westminster is a good center around which to cluster the great churches of Europe; Manchester is a center for the discussion of manufacturing cities. The children are old enough to do good reference work. Recitations come on alternate days. In Europe especially, history, literature, tradition, and myth play almost as significant a role as the present facts.

Second Term. Winter.

The silk industry at Lyons. (Silkworms, trade in silk).

Grape culture. (Bordeaux, wine, shipping).

The Rhine. (Scenery, churches, history, commerce, ruins).

The German army. (Drill, recruits, maneuvers, barracks).

Out-door life in Germany. (Gardens, music, concerts, walks).

The sugar beet. (Raising the crop, the mill, the refinery).

The public schools. The University of Berlin.

Amsterdam and the dikes of Holland. (History).

The Alps. (Surface, scenery, rivers, lakes, people, tunnels).

Genoa and Venice. (History, location, and buildings).

"Modern Europe" in The World and its People series will be very useful as a reference. Bædeker's guide books will be helpful for details. Frye's Geography also.

Let the children study and interpret the wall maps, and explain the surface features of Europe as a whole; also, draw the maps in outline on board and paper. Frequent comparisons with important topics treated in the United States will be valuable for both the old and new. Notice the variety of languages and races in Europe, and the fact that emigrants from Europe have settled in all parts of our country.

Third Term. Spring.

Rome. (St. Peters, The Coliseum, The Vatican ruins).
The Alhambra at Granada, The Acropolis at Athens.
The Mediterranean Sea. (Historical stories and references).
The Danube. (Variety of races, cities, and languages).
The four seas of Russia. (Cities and commerce).
The Czar. (Moscow, Peter the Great, The Kremlin).
Hammerfest. (Arctic land and people).
The Peninsulas of Europe (Surface, people, climate).
The Gulf Stream. (Effects on climate and products).

The whole year's work for Europe should be kept in mind while teaching any term's topics. It is not expected in the plan of geography to spend much time in formal reviews, but by means of significant comparisons of city with city, river with river, government of England with government of Russia, etc., constantly review and make use of our previous stores of knowledge. The old standards or types may be used again and again, both helping and interpreting the new topics, and reviewing the old from new standpoints. Reference books of travel, guide books, historical places of great interest, and the points suggested by other studies need careful attention. Structural ideas and commercial routes on a large scale deserve notice and comparison with similar things in America.

Natural Science.

In the sixth grade a large number of important topics are suggested by the geography, history, and literature, but these suggestions will not suffice for a full course. The age and previous science studies, combined with the general development of nature lore will suggest many suitable topics. Besides the topics of regular study in this year, the previous observations along the line of plant and animal life, of mineral and physical objects, should be kept up and reviewed incidentally in the form of comparisons, contrasts, leading to larger grasp of classifications. Life histories and life groups should be traced out and the broader laws underlying the variety of life and phenomena understood so far as they can be inferred by the children from the facts well observed. Depend as little as possible upon facts derived from books. Encourage close and regular observation and the collection and examination of specimens so far as they have a clear purpose and meaning.

First Term. Fall.

The grasshopper (continued, locust, cricket).

Common weeds. Shepherd's purse, rag weed, meadow parsnip, field sorrel.

Animal life in brooks and ponds. "Up and Down the Brooks."

The butterfly (continued, life history, migrations).

The house fly.

The ocean, depth, saltiness, storms, temperature, icebergs, ocean currents, animal life in the sea, corals.

Water and its *impurities,* disinfectants, soap.

Teachers can get a large amount of information on these topics from books, and many suggestions as to method of study, but they should be sparing of their direct gifts of information to children. Let both teacher and pupil examine, investigate, and work out their conclusions. Give written and oral tests: drawing is also a good means of sharpening observation and testing knowledge.

Second Term. Winter.

The telegraph, telephone, history of electricity.

Sugar in plants, grape, beet, cane, maple, fruits; physical and chemical processes in extracting and refining.

The ear, instruments of music, sound, vibrations.

Internal organs and *bony structure* of fish, bird, rabbit.

Volcanoes of Europe, history, internal heat, crust of the earth.

Hydrostatics and hydraulics.

Processes in *glassmaking, porcelain*.

A number of these topics admit of illustrative devices in the laboratory, others must be made clear by means of diagrams and descriptions. Even in those topics not admitting of objective illustration, clearness of thought and power to reason should be exercised.

Third Term. Spring.

Continue the study of internal organs and structure in animals. The *frog*, the *cray-fish*, the *earthworm*. The life history, internal organs, and structure of each should be aimed at.

Animal life in *brooks* and *ponds* may be continued into the spring and summer.

The ant, life in communities, nests. mode of life. Forests and forest preservation. Trees of Europe.

Animal life in Europe, the *hare*, reindeer, chamois, the stork, robin red breast, pigeon.

Continue the study of common weeds in spring.

The children have now collected enough experience to begin to see the family groups in nature, and the laws that prevail in plant and animal life.

Books of Reference in Sixth Grade Science.

Ants, Bees and Wasps (Lubbock). D. Appleton & Co.

Up and Down the Brooks (Bamford). Houghton, Mifflin & Co.

The Beauties of Nature (Lubbock). Macmillan.

Any good text book in Physics or Natural Philosophy.

Elements of Biology (Boyer). D. C. Heath & Co.

The Life of a Butterfly (Scudder). Henry Holt & Co.

Flower and Fruit, Part II (Newell). Ginn & Co.

Town Geology (Kingsley). Macmillan & Co.

Romance of the Insect World (Badenoch). Macmillan & Co.

How to Study Plants (Wood). A. S. Barnes & Co., Chicago.

Manual of the Apiary (Cook). Thos. G. Newman & Son, Chicago.

A Reader in Botany (Newell), Part I. Ginn & Co.

Worms and Crustacea, No. VII. D. C. Heath.

Common Hydroids, Corals and Echinoderms, No. V. D. C. Heath & Co.

Nature Study (Jackman). Henry Holt & Co.

The Great World's Farm (Gaye). Seeley & Co. (Macmillan).

Science for All. Four volumes.

Arithmetic.

The work of this year involves a review of common fractions, decimals, and compound numbers.

Some of the chief things to be attained are as follows:

The power in children to think and see through problems and the application of principles for themselves.

A quick, ready mastery of the elementary facts of arithmetic in both oral and written work so that children can feel that they are accurate and reliable.

Whatever mechanical drills are necessary should be rapid and energetic, up to the full measure of children's powers.

After a principle has been clearly grasped by inductive reasoning, let the children read the problems thoughtfully and apply the principle rationally (not mechanically).

Give plenty of oral drill, making up problems from the common objects about the school and town.

In compound numbers, measure and test the standards in a great variety of ways. Estimate objects with the standard units as a basis. In arithmetic train children to test and prove their own work and be self reliant. Do not lose sight of principles in the multitude of problems. Consult Cook's Methods in Written Arithmetic.

First Term. Fall.

A complete review of fractions, common and decimal. Let children make the tables of compound numbers from the standard units. Make the measurements and give oral problems till the relations are clear and sure. Take examples from objects treated in the other studies, throwing light also upon those studies.

Work out in a sequence the areas of rectangles, parallelograms, triangles, and the contents of prisms. Get areas of walls, ceilings, and floors of rooms, etc. Master factoring, greatest common divisor, and least common multiple before trying to apply them to fractions. Children blunder through fractions for lack of power to quickly analyze numbers into their factors.

Use diagrams and make sketches on the board.

Second Term. Winter.

In this and the next term's work the whole of the previous work in arithmetic should be summed up and mastered up to percentage. Children should see clearly how closely all the parts of their previous work hang together. The mechanical exercises may be so mastered that pupils will feel confident in their strength, and grasp always at the principle of a problem, rather than at some mechanical device for solving it. Give variety to every lesson. Keep the whole class busy. Do not assign long lessons, but insist upon regularity and completeness of work.

Third Term. Spring.

Complete the review of arithmetic up to percentage, working oral problems with speed and applying the principles to more difficult problems in fractions and compound numbers. Study Cook's Methods in Written Arithmetic.

Language.

In this grade, the exercises in the use of correct English, oral and written, should be brought to completion. Up to this point the children have had great variety of drill in speaking and writing. It is only reasonable to expect that at the end of this grade they have the mastery of the irregular forms of verbs, pronouns, inflections, etc., readiness in correct written work, in spelling, punctuation, use of abbreviations, capitals, etc., and the forms of letter writing and composition. There should be great care in the oral use of correct forms of language in all classes of this grade. The language lessons, especially, should review completely all the previous exercises in correct forms, and the other lessons should closely apply the lessons.

First Term. Fall.

The purpose in this grade as in previous years is not to teach technical grammar, but correct practice. Spend little or no time in grammatical terms and distinctions. Use Bright's Graded Instruction in English, seventh grade, but omit the grammar. Review carefully the exercises in fifth and sixth grades. The other lessons furnish materials for intelligent exercises in composition. Let the language teacher notice the work in history, natural science, and geography for composition topics. and for thought materials for language drill.

Second Term. Winter.

Take the language drills in Bright's for seventh grade. Suitable composition exercises are furnished by the books read outside of school, biographical sketches, science lessons, etc. Train to a regular use of the dictionary. Special drills are necessary in dictionary exercises. Let the written work be held to neatness and correctness of form.

Third Term. Spring.

Review irregular verbs, homonyms, derivations, abbreviations, rules of spelling. Use Bright as a whole through eighth grade exercises. Keep up the use of the dictionary. Preserve the compositions and note progress in original natural expression.

Drawing.

Bring the drawing exercises into close relation to the geography, reading, natural science, and history. Public buildings, monuments, and works of art in our own country and in Europe will furnish some suitable lessons. Some of the public buildings of the home city will also furnish illustrations of style in architecture and ornament.

Read Miss Stoker's plan for drawing in "Seeing and Doing." Notice the course laid out suggestively for sixth grade. Study the work of the other sixth grade lessons for the year, and notice where the drawing may help in observation and clearer grasp of ideas. The principles of drawing as an art may be brought out in these drawing exercises. Let the children deal in realities and try to express what they see. Do not waste time in bare formal descriptions or language exercises as a preliminary to drawing. Watch the children closely and individually at their work, and correct and guard against faults and errors. Some of the drawings may well be preserved and used to illustrate, in regular series, the work in other studies.

Writing.

Careful drill should be given in the mastery and use of the vertical script. Follow the plan laid down by Mr. Cavins for third grade, modifying it suitably for upper grade. Do not accept poor and careless work. Reject it entirely and call for reasonable neatness and care. Encourage children to so far master the writing as to be excused from it at the earliest date. Let the writing teacher observe the character of the written work in other studies and report to the critic teachers. Skill and efficiency in one study should be realized in other studies where it may be applied. Notice especially the compositions and exercises in language. For writing exercises copy some choice passages from the best authors and preserve. Be careful to prevent blots on paper, desks, and floor.

Spelling.

The spelling words are drawn from the other studies. Notice carefully the plan outlined for third grade. Write the words in the spelling blank with ink and exercise care in neat vertical writing. Pronounce words clearly and but once, as a rule. Be sure that the meaning of the words is clear to the pupils. Correct the spelling lists very carefully. Report careless and backward pupils regularly to the room teacher, but first use every reasonable effort to secure good work before depending upon others. Notice all simple rules and analogies in spelling. Keep desks neat and clean, writing materials in order, and spelling books without marks and blots.

Music.

In upper intermediate grades, let the children learn some new classic songs, suited to the age of the children, the season, and the devotional exercises. Consult the "Model Music Course," Second and Third Readers. Let the children learn the words after they have been read and discussed in class. Drill exercises in music are also furnished in the music readers.

The Model Music Course is published by The John Church Company, of Cincinnati, New York, and Chicago.

SEVENTH GRADE.

In the seventh school year we make the epoch of the Revolution the center of the historical studies, and also of many of the classic and historical materials used in reading lessons. Other reading matter is also derived from the colonial period and from the history and literature of Europe. The children are now advanced enough to receive a strong impression from this great epoch of history and from the classic masterpieces which are, in some cases, closely related to the history. In language they are prepared for a genuine entrance into grammar. A term's work in composition leading up to grammar may well begin the language work of the year. In geography, having completed the geography of Europe, they are ready to move out to the geography of the rest of the world, completing this study by the end of the year. The natural science lessons will remain related in many natural ways to the geography, history, and literature, although it must grow more independent in pursuit of the aims of science as we advance in the grades. The arithmetic will give a mastery of percentage and its applications, and needs to be extensively related to the subject matter of other studies.

In order to produce a natural and legitimate connection of all the studies of this year, it will be necessary for each teacher of a subject to make a comprehensive and somewhat detailed study of the whole year's work of the class. In many cases it will help greatly to examine closely the work of the preceding year and the real status of the class.

It is impossible to advance properly in any study without constant use of previous year's work. This is especially true in arithmetic and the incidental reviews and comparisons of the main topics of study with those previously studied in geography, history, natural science, and reading are the most valuable exercises for training children to think, reason, and make use of their knowledge.

Each teacher, besides the general plan and work for the whole class, should have an appreciative eye for the individualities of the pupils, for their personal traits, disposition, ability, or weakness. The room teacher and the teacher in reading, as well as others, may afford to watch the tastes of children in the reading of library books or in their other outside employments during leisure hours. An effort to appreciate and understand personal character as it shows itself in a great variety of forms, is one of those things of vital moment in the teacher's work, but is very apt to be neglected.

Reading.

The masterpieces selected for this year are largely of our American writers and cluster about the Revolution, the most thrilling period of our national history. But many of the works selected reach well back into the colonial period. Several of the best selections are English classics suited to pupils of this age.

The reading teacher should make a study of the Special Method in Reading as a preparation for the spirit and method of the work, but, more important still, is the earnest, sympathetic reading and re-reading of the classics themselves. These are real treasures, whose great value comes to the consciousness after several readings. Let every teacher cultivate his taste, imagination and social nature upon these choice materials of thought and expression. For the teacher to thoroughly appreciate and enjoy these masterpieces is a great step toward preparation for the reading lessons. Every teacher of this grade should survey the materials of literature adapted to this year, and make as close and extensive acquaintance with it as possible. The introduction of complete classics in the place of the readers will not meet serious objection if carried out gradually and prudently. Shorter classic poems and masterpieces are not neglected, but many will be memorized or read in connection with the other larger works.

First Term. Fall.

Evangeline, Houghton, Mifflin & Co.

Tales of Shakespeare (Lamb), Ginn & Co.; also Macmillan & Co.

Washington's Rules of Conduct, letters, etc., for sight and home reading. Houghton, Mifflin & Co.; Maynard, Merrill & Co.

The Declaration of Independence, Old South Leaflets, D. C. Heath & Co.

For home reading we may use Stories of Our Country, American Book Co., and Peasant and Prince, Ginn & Co.

The historical references will prove interesting if traced out. The Tales of Shakespeare will prove an interesting introduction to the plays themselves, some of which, in selections, may be read in connection with the stories.

Second Term. Winter.

Sella, Thanatopsis, and other poems, Houghton, Mifflin & Co., especially the patriotic selections.

Grandmother's Story of Bunker Hill, etc., Houghton, Mifflin & Co.

Tales of the White Hills, Houghton, Mifflin & Co.

For sight reading use Poor Richard's Almanac, Houghton, Mifflin & Co., and Rab and His Friends, Home Book Co., and Maynard, Merrill & Co.

In connection with the classics study the lives and characters of the authors. The library furnishes good reference material for both teachers and pupils. References for children's use should be definite and not too extensive. Paul Revere's Ride, Under the Old Elm, and Emerson's poem on the battle of Lexington also belong to this term's work.

Third Term. Spring.

Bunker Hill Monument (speech by Webster). Ginn & Co., Houghton, Mifflin.

Enoch Arden and the Lotus Eaters. Maynard, Merrill & Co.

The Christmas Carol, Houghton, Mifflin & Co.

For sight and collateral reading use Sharp Eyes and other papers. Houghton, Mifflin & Co. and The Succession of Forest Trees, Houghton, Mifflin & Co.

For home reading recommend Silas Marner, Rob Roy, and The Two Great Retreats.

Keep up the practice of memorizing short poems and select passages from the longer classics. Frequently it is well to read a classic through a second time with a class after carefully going over it once. The comparison of passages in different poems and from different authors is a source of thoughtfulness and interest. Notice striking or beautiful figures of speech. Cultivate a taste for the esthetic elements in literature. Observe how far the habit of reading classics even outside the school work may be cultivated in average children. Do not spend too much time in discussion but secure a large amount of vigorous, oral reading in the class.

History.

In studying the period of the Revolution, begin with biography and make the personal interest in two or three leading characters the means of a spirited and instructive entrance upon the struggle of the Revolution. The important thing for a teacher is to select wisely a few important topics and gather about them abundance of descriptive detail, showing causal relations and binding together into a network a large body of historical facts.

The recitations will come on alternate days and, beside the text-book used, the children should read in biography and history on important topics, according to definite assignments made by the teacher. The life of Washington, the life of Samuel Adams, and a few main campaigns and topics of the war will be the centers of study with which all the ideas will be associated. The literature of the year stands in very close relation to the history and the light thrown upon one by the other should be made good use of. The moral and patriotic suggestions contained in these historical and literary materials may be strongly felt by the pupils.

Study the plan for seventh grade history outlined in the Special Method in Literature and History.

First Term. Fall.

Scudder's Life of Washington. Houghton, Mifflin & Co.

Let this book be the basis for this term's work. If children have previously studied the early life of Washington, this part may be abridged or passed over more rapidly. That part relating to the events in Virginia at the opening of the Revolutionary struggle may be made important and detailed. Some reference work on Patrick Henry and other patriots of Virginia may be in place here. In treating the life of Washington, his own campaigns about Boston, New York, and Philadelphia should be brought out more fully. Use maps freely, and diagrams to illustrate campaigns and battles.

Second Term. Winter.

Finish the Life of Washington to the close of the Revolution. Study for a month or six weeks the life of Samuel Adams and the opening events of the Revolution about Boston. Let the teacher handle the subject in part orally, using such definite reference work as may be appropriate to the children. Much of the literature of this epoch clusters about Boston. Each pupil should keep a note-book in which to arrange in orderly manner the leading topics discussed orally and by reference work in the class. Let the leading topics be well mastered and arranged in orderly form by each pupil.

Third Term. Spring.

The leading topics for the spring study are as follows: Burgoyne's invasion, presented orally by the teacher. Much collateral reference work may be done by the pupils. Let the teacher use Burgoyne's Invasion, by S. A. Drake: Lee & Shepard. Cornwallis' campaign at the South and Yorktown, also presented orally by the teacher, with definite reference work. State of money matters at the close of the war, and the growing hostility between the states.

The Philadelphia convention and the framing of the constitution. For the last two topics, John Fiske's Critical Period of American History will furnish the best book for the teacher's use. Let the teacher master and present the chief points. Let the pupils be held for a good reproduction of the topics presented and discussed, for careful reference study and for neat outlines in their note-books of work done.

Geography.

The seventh grade geography includes the leading type studies of Asia, Australia, Africa, South America, and the world-whole, and completes the regular course in this study.

A few important topics are taken as important centers and types. Europe is the starting point for the geographical movement into the great continent and oceans not yet studied in detail. All the topics taken up for full treatment in this grade are new, although frequent comparisons with somewhat similar topics in North America and Europe will be very suggestive and instructive. In treating such continents as Asia, Australia, Africa, and South America brief attention should be called to historical topics and persons of special interest, as Livingston and Stanley in Africa, Clive and Hastings and the missionairies, Cary and Judson, in India, the penal colonies of Australia, Pizarro in Peru, etc. These persons suggest suitable books of travel, conquest and missionary work for home reading.

Frye's Complete Geography and the geographical readers and books of travel will be of great service to the teacher. Much of the work will have to be done by oral presentation, but much reference study can be laid upon the pupils if books are available. Let each pupil keep an outline book for recording the main things in outline at least. Outline map drawing should be practiced regularly. Written and oral tests should help to secure systematic mastery of topics.

At the close of the year's work there should be a broad survey of the commercial, structural, and climatic regions of the world. The distribution of population into civilized, semi-civilized, etc., should be observed.

First Term. Fall.

The following type studies are suggested:

The *Suez Canal* and the Route from England to India.

British India as a Colonial Possession (history, government).

The *Religion of India* and *China* (caste system, missions, temples, sacred rivers).

The *Himalaya Mountains*. (The physical structure of Asia, slopes and rivers, deserts and climate).

The *Rice Fields* (food of the people).

Tea Culture.(cultivation, picking, boxing and shipping).

The *Yangste River* and the System of Internal Commerce (variety of boats, canals, Shanghai and other cities as trade centers).

The *Over-land Trade-route* from Irkutsk to Moscow.

The *People of Japan* (their character, manufactures, adoption of modern ideas, the recent war, commerce).

Java, a Tropical Island (products, people, government, commerce).

The central idea of each important type must be clearly grasped and the facts gathered about this to explain its meaning. Otherwise there is danger of loose and scattering work by both pupils and teacher. Leave out many things for the sake of a clear explanation of a few.

Second Term. Winter.

Sheep Ranches in *Australia* (grass, rabbits, climate).

New Zealand as a British settlement and colony.

The *Indian Ocean* (currents, trade winds, commercial routes, islands, neighboring shores, peoples, entering rivers).

The *Nile River* (floods, history, ruins, cities, people).

The *Desert of Sahara* (sandy wastes, caravans, oases, Bedouin tribes; compare with deserts of Central Asia).

Negroes of Central Africa (villages, climate, slave trade).

The Congo River. Tropical Africa.
An Ostrich Farm in Cape Colony.
The Diamond fields of South Africa.

Besides the full treatment of these topics, old type studies begun in other countries should be extended by additions and comparisons, *e.g.*, the gold mines of Australia compared with those of California; the climate, products, etc., of the East Indies compared with those of the West Indies; the lakes of Africa likened to those of North America; the Falls of the Zambezi recalled with Niagara; the slopes and rivers of Siberia compared with those of the Mackenzie, etc. The reviews by means of comparison are more interesting and instructive than simple repetitions, and they lead to thoughtfulness and use of previous knowledge as well as to system and classification.

Third Term. Spring.

A Cattle Ranch on the LaPlata.
A Coffee Plantation in Brazil.
The Amazon. Tropical river and forest.
The Andes (the backbone of a continent, comparisons).
The Pacific Ocean (size, islands, trade routes).
The Sandwich Islands.
The Nicaragua Canal (shortening of trade routes).
The Anglo-Saxon Race (its spread and influence).
Distribution of Land and Water upon the globe.
Mathematical Geography, latitude and longitude, seasons, zones.

It is advisable that we make the type studies of the United States and North America a series of *standards* upon which to measure the rest of the continents, rivers, productions, industries, peoples, etc. This will give constant review from new standpoints, and will link all the parts of geography during the successive years closely into one body of knowledge. But there is great danger that such oral lessons as we have suggested may prove loose, incomplete, and unsystematic. The work should be clear and comprehensive, and be thoroughly mastered. The note-books should show the careful and orderly quality of the work. The following plan and outline for Composition and Grammar in seventh and eighth grades is prepared by Miss Kate Mavity of the Training Department of the Normal School.

Composition and Grammar.

OUTLINE.

First term.—Composition—lessons every other day.

Second term.—Grammar and Composition—lessons every day.

First Month.

a. { A thought process—the three elements.
   { A sentence—the three elements.

b. { Simple, complex, and compound thoughts.
   { Simple, complex, and compound sentences.

c. One composition.

Second Month.

a. { Objects, attributes, and relations.
   { Substantives, attributives, and relationals.

b. One composition.

Third Month.

a. { Simple ideas, groups of ideas, and thought processes.
   { Words, phrases, and clauses distinguished.

b. Words classed into substantive, attributive, and relational. Nouns, pronouns, and infinitives defined.

c. One composition.

Third term.—Grammar and Composition—lessons every day.

First Month.

a. The attributive parts of speech defined.

b. The relational parts of speech defined.

c. Phrases.

d. One composition.

Second Month.

a. Modifiers.
b. Clauses.
c. One composition.

Third Month.

a. Analysis of a classic selection.
b. One composition.

The Composition Work.

The first term of the seventh year is to be given entirely to work in composition. It is supposed that the pupils have been writing compositions ever since they were able to write and have had considerable practice in expressing their thoughts on paper. Facility in writing letters and compositions has already been acquired and the language habits of the pupils are firmly fixed.

The recitations in seventh grade, occur every other day, giving the pupils in all about thirty-five lessons.

Three things are to be accomplished in this work: first, to give the pupils a working knowledge of how to compose; second, to drill in applying the discovered law; and third, to get the class into readiness for the grammar work and to lay the basis for it.

In writing the first composition it would be well to have the teacher and pupils together select the subject, and in doing so the teacher can lead the pupils to see what a good subject is. Subjects will be rejected because they are too broad, are worn out, or not clearly stated, while the one chosen will be selected because of its interest, unity, clearness, etc.

The children should gather material on the selected subject and bring it to the class for discussion. There it will be sorted and important and unimportant points be distinguished.

The next recitation might arrange the material according to the purpose of the composition. This completes the organization of the composition.

The teacher should caution the children before they begin to write to see 'that every sentence is complete, and clear; that they use the best words to express their meaning; that each paragraph holds one topic; and that they vary the expression. Punctuation and capitalization should have been well looked after long before this time, but if the pupils have not already formed good habits in these lines the teacher will have to direct them about these points.

In drilling in applying the points worked out in the first composition, it is not at all necessary that the pupils all write upon the same subject. Each one may choose his own subject with the sanction of his teacher. This gives opportunity for encouraging the true writer's spirit, individual interest in some special thing, and the desire to awaken the same interest in others.

The compositions should be read and discussed as to excellence or the reverse, and the pupils should be asked to judge which one gave the most practical information, was most thoroughly enjoyed, or was best fitted to inspire to higher living, according to the purpose of the composition.

Here is an excellent opportunity to bring the pupils to the correct view of the relation thought and language bear to each other; and this, well understood, would completely do away with "wordy" compositions, and would serve as an excellent foundation for the work in grammar which is to follow.

About ten compositions can be written during the first term's work, and one will be written each month during the remainder of the seventh and during the eighth year. The monthly compositions will not require more than one or two recitation periods, as the pupils can prepare them and have them ready to read before the teacher needs to give special time to them.

The subjects and materials for composition will come largely from the other branches of study, or they will be suggested by points in their other lessons.

The Grammar Work.

The first month's work in grammar aims to take the pupil up two steps of the grammar stairs:—to give him a clear insight into the nature and essential elements of the sentence, and to lead him to distinguish sentences as simple, complex, and compound. Both of these points grow directly out of an understanding of a thought process and its three necessary ideas. A thought is the unit of thinking. The mind has no "sense" unless it has a complete thought. The process that the mind goes through with in thinking a thought, we call a thought process. In every thought process there are three ideas,—the idea of an object, the idea of an attribute, and the idea of whether the attribute belongs to the object. This will be seen by the pupil when he has examined a number of thoughts carefully under the supervision of the teacher. He should have a large number and a great variety to generalize from. He should try to see if he can think one in which it is not true, and everything necessary should be done to make the point a *sure* one.

A sentence is the expression of a thought. When we express a thought, we have three ideas that must be expressed. There must be a language form to express the idea of the object, one to express the idea of the attribute, and something to express the idea of the relation between them. So every sentence will have three elements, its subject, its predicate, its copula. The subject, predicate, and copula should be defined on the basis of special function in expressing the thought. The point should be made that some times the same language form may express both attribute and relation, therefore may be both predicate and copula. Sufficient drill should be given in finding the three elements in sentences to make the pupils ready and accurate in recognizing them.

A thought is simple when it consists of a single thought process. It is complex when it consists of two or more unequal thought processes. It is compound when it consists of two or more equal thought processes. Knowing what a thought process is, it will be quite easy for the pupil to see that there are two or more in certain thoughts that he examines. And, of course, if he understands simple, complex, and compound thoughts, he will see the necessity for clauses of equal and unequal importance in sentences, and consequently have a working knowledge of the corresponding classes of sentences.

We try to approach an understanding of all language forms by examining the thought forms that necessitate them. When the pupil sees a real demand for something that will express the idea of an object, the substantive language form has a value to him and therefore he does not forget about it. It has a work to do, and seems a useful, almost a live, thing to him.

There are only three things in the world—objects, attributes, and relations. Every thing is one of these three. Consequently we have only three kinds of ideas—ideas of objects, of attributes, and of relations. What is an object? One of the first duties of the teacher is to wipe out the erroneous impression that only those things are objects that can be perceived by the five senses. If that were true, then all objects would be physical and a large number of our nouns, such as "opinion," "idea," "belief," "joy," "sorrow," etc. are not the names of objects. If not of objects, of what? Objects are both spiritual and physical. Anything that the mind examines to find attributes of is an object. When the mind centers its activities upon anything, that thing is an object. The mind can turn an attribute into an object by giving its attention to the attribute and thinking something about it.

An attribute is a phase or property of an object. It has no individual existence of its own, but is only there for its value to the thing to which it belongs.

Relation is the connection between things. It is what makes the mind consider two things together in the same thought. Relations are of many varieties—time, place, cause, similarity, relation of attribute to object, etc.

Lively drills should be given in recognizing objects of all kinds, attributes of all kinds, and relations of all kinds.

We think about objects and therefore need language forms to express our ideas of them. Those language forms are called substantive. The pupil should be drilled in recognizing substantives — not substantive *words* alone, but phrases and clauses. No distinction need be made between the kinds of forms.

Attributives and relationals may be approached in the same manner. Words having double functions, as the attributive verb, which expresses an attribute of action and relation also, and the relative pronoun, should be brought up so that the pupil may see that words may express two kinds of ideas and that *what they express* determines their classification.

A simple idea is a single idea; the mind goes through only one change in thinking it, as the idea "red." The words "dark red" express an idea of color but it is not a simple idea; the mind has two simple ideas in thinking that complex one.

The mind forms its simple ideas into groups which are themselves either complex or compound ideas. Words express simple ideas, while those language forms that express the groups we call phrases. When we find a thought process within a thought we use a clause to express it.

Simple ideas of objects are expressed by substantive words. A substantive word may name its object or it may express it without naming it. Those that name we call nouns; those that do not name, pronouns. When the mind makes an attribute of action into an object and names it we call the name an infinitive.

When a simple idea of an attribute needs expression we use an attributive word. If the attribute belongs to an object, the word expressing it is an adjective in its nature; if the attribute belongs to another attribute or to a relation, the word is adverbial in its nature. The adjective, the attributive verb, the participle, and the interjection are adjective attributives.

The adjective expresses the attribute but cannot relate it to the object—it is *purely* attributive. The attributive verb is different from the adjective only in having the assertive or relational element. On account of its having this copulative function, the attributive verb can never be a modifier as the adjective can, but will always express two of the principal ideas in the thought process, that is, it is the predicate adjective *and* the verb. The participle is the active action adjective. The interjection always expresses the attribute of condition belonging to the mind of the author of the sentence.

The verb is always the principal relational in the sentence. It has for its work the expressing of the relation between the object which the subject expresses and the predicate attribute. "Is" is the pure, the typical verb. Whenever we find the "is" function in a word, it is a verb. We see now why "The verb is the life of the sentence." We cannot have a sentence without a verb, for we can have no thought process without thinking the relation between the object and the attribute, and *this relation* is the *meaning* of the word "*is.*" The preposition expresses relation of time, place, purpose, etc., between unequal ideas. It is always found in a phrase, which phrase expresses an attribute belonging to the thing expressed by the word that the phrase modifies. The conjunction expresses the relation between equal ideas or thought processes. It shades off into the preposition.

A phrase is a group of words expressing a group of ideas; or, we might say, expressing a complex or compound idea. Phrases, like words, are of three kinds;—those expressing ideas of objects, those expressing ideas of attributes, and those expressing ideas of relation. Substantive phrases may be noun, pronoun, or infinitive phrases, according to the functions they perform. Clausal phrases are usually substantive, though they may express an attribute of cause or reason about a verbal relation. A clausal phrase expresses a thought process, but slights the relation either by not expressing it at all or by using a participle or an infinitive instead of a verb. It is just like a clause, except that the clause expresses its relation with a verb: hence its name. Attributive phrases have the same classification as attributive words.

The so-called prepositional phrase is not really prepositional, but is always attributive, either adjective or adverbial. The most important relational phrase is the copulative or verbal phrase, which expresses the principal relation in the thought. Its principal word is always the verb, which may be modified by adverbs of negation, time, or cause. The *real* prepositional phrase is purely relational. Its principal word is a preposition whose relation is modified by an attribute expressed by an adverb, as, "nearly to," "almost across," "just beyond," etc.

So long as only words and simple ideas are discussed, no questions as to modification and modifiers will arise. But a study of phrases reveals principal and subordinate elements. All the words within the group are not of equal value in expressing the complex idea. Some words belong to other words; they are there simply to help the other words express a definite idea. Considerable drill needs to be given in distinguishing the different kinds of modifiers.

Clauses are old friends of the pupil. He had them in connection with complex and compound sentences and he has met with them off and on ever since. The only new point is the classification on the basis of content into substantive and attributive. Attributive clauses are either adjective or adverbial. The pupil has ample basis for making this classification.

By analyzing a classic selection we mean examining it to see what language forms the author uses to express his thought. The analysis should not be all formal or mechanical.

Arithmetic.

The arithmetic work of the seventh grade will consist of a review in the fall term and of a careful study of percentage during the rest of the year. The lack of efficiency and thoroughness in arithmetic make it necessary to repeat work several times in order to secure a reasonable mastery. Let the teacher in the seventh grade make a study of Cook's Methods in written arithmetic and learn the suggestions, forms of board work in classes, methods of testing, devices for securing thought rather than mechanical effort, accuracy of language and clear explanation. Let the teacher have a clear aim in every lesson and push steadily toward it. More time is wasted in arithmetic than would be needed in mastering it. Be clear and pointed in illustration, question, and requirement. Throw children upon their own thought power after giving them the direction and materials of thought.

First Term. Fall.

Review the elements of arithmetic, give plenty of oral drills. Take common and decimal fractions, compound numbers, and tests of divisibility. Complete the review up to percentage.

The following plan and suggestions for teaching percentage in the winter and spring term of seventh grade are worked out by Mr. J. A. Keith, of the Normal School. The text used in the class is Cook and Cropsey's Advanced Arithmetic. But a great variety of oral problems, especially simple applications to familiar measures and objects are made up by the teacher for each class. Many other written problems are also needed beyond what the book furnishes. Any such plan as is here outlined is necessarily fragmentary.

Percentage.

GENERAL PLAN.

1. *Object*, or unit of thought.

(*a*). Any quantity or number (measure of material or thought quantity) may be considered as consisting of one hundred equal parts, commensurable or incommensurable.

(*b*). Any quantity or number may be compared with any like quantity or number to find (1) what part the first is of the second, (2) how many times the first the second is. In each case the relation is a *ratio*, and may be expressed by making the consequent 100. The first number thus becomes some number of hundredths of the second.

(*c*). Any quantity or number may be considered as some number of *hundredths* of a quantity or number to be found.

Hence, three *cases* or *problems* in percentage arise:

1. To find any per cent of any quantity or number.
2. To find what per cent one quantity or number is of a like quantity or number.

3. To find a quantity or number some per cent of which is given.

In (1) a two-fold process is implied—*a*, finding one per cent of the given number; *b*, multiplying this result by the given per cent. This should present no difficulty.

In (2) we find what part the first is of the second and express it as a fraction. Reduce this fraction to hundredths. The number of hundredths is the number of per cent which the first is of the second. Another method is to find one per cent of the second number and divide the first by it.

In (3) we have to find one per cent of the required number by division, and multiply this result by 100.

The pupils are supposed to be familiar with all the technical work here outlined. If any review of elementary arithmetic be necessary, it should be conducted with an eye single to the percentage relations. The *only* new fact is: any quantity or number is made up of one hundred equal parts. The difficult task is to understand the relations of this fact to the whole body of arithmetical knowledge previously acquired—to comprehend the complex relations produced by this one fact.

II. *The aim:* (*a*) To understand the percentage relations; (*b*) to express these relations in truthful language; (*c*) to acquire facility in solution of problems.

III. *Steps* by which the aim is to be realized.

(*a*) Thinking.
 1. Concrete quantitative illustrations.
 2. Concrete number illustrations.
 3. Absolute relations.

(*b*) Doing.
 1. With objects.
 2. With thought objects (concrete numbers).
 3. With number relations.
 4. Drill.

SPECIAL PLANS. CASE II.
I.

I. *Aim:* (1) To teach that any object may be considered as made up of one hundred equal parts. (2) What these equal parts are called. (3) How any number of these equal parts may be expressed.

II. *Method:* An apple will be presented to the class; it will be cut into halves, fourths, and eighths. The pupils will be required to tell what part of the apple, peeling, meat, juice, etc., is presented each time. The pupils will be told that the apple and each element of the apple is made up of one hundred equal parts. Each of these parts is what part of the whole? The fractional parts of the apple will be presented again, and questions regarding the number of hundredths of the apple, peeling, meat, juice, etc., in each part will be asked.

III. These facts and statements will be give.

1. *Per cent* means by the hundred. Six per cent means six hundredths. ($6 \div 100 = \frac{6}{100}$.)

2. *Per cent* may be expressed in four ways, viz.:
    1. Words—Ten per cent.
    2. Sign—6 %, six %.
    3. Common fraction—$\frac{6}{100}$.
    4. Decimal fraction—.06.

Pupils will be required to express, in these four ways, the parts of apple, peeling, etc., presented them as *per cent* of apple, peeling, etc.

[A meter stick may be used to good advantage in developing the points in this lesson.]

IV. *Assignment for second lesson.*

Four equivalent circles will be drawn upon the board, divided into parts of various sizes, and lettered. Questions relating to these areas will be put on the board. $A = \frac{1}{2}$ circle. $B = \frac{1}{4}$ circle. $B : A?$ B is what per cent of A? $A : B?$ A is what per cent of B?

II.

I. Oral review of yesterday's work.

II. Have pupils read results of their home work, pointing out the areas compared.

III. Advance *aim:* To find the per cent relations existing between some measures of length.

IV. *Method:* A foot ruler divided into inches will be used. *Questions illustrating method:* (1) 1 in. : 1 ft.? (2) 1 in. is how many hundredths of 1 ft.? (3) 1 in. is how many per cent of 1 ft.? Take many concrete problems of this kind, for you can get the entire class to think. Make up a list and solve them yourself. Keep away from the text-books awhile. We take up this case of percentage first, because it seems logical that the child should pass from decimals and measure to their combined application.

Any teacher can state aims for the subsequent work. Review compound numbers in this way. Do not fear to be original in devices. Pupils do not acquire the new *habit* implied in this work very readily. Do not forget that the first number is some part of the second. Be sure that pupils see this relation. A week or more spent on this kind of work is very profitably spent. Insist on accuracy. Change the problems by putting the second number in place of the first. If pupils do not already know it, teach that a fraction may mean one of two things. Ex.—$\frac{5}{6}$ means (1) five of the six equal parts into which a unit is divided; (2) one-sixth of five units.

PLAN III. CASE I.

I. *Aim:* To find 27 per cent of the volume of a solid 8 in. long, 4 in. wide, and 4 in. thick.

II. *Method:* The class will find the volume in cu. in. of the solid presented. You are to find what part of the volume of this solid? "27 per cent." Express this part as *hundredths* of the volume of the solid. "27 *hundredths.*"

How will you proceed to find 27 per cent of the volume of this solid? Now find 13 per cent, 19 per cent, 47 per cent, 53 per cent, 79 per cent, etc., of the volume of the solid. The meter-stick will be used in developing the quantitative phase of this work.

The following will be the form of the work:

27 per cent of 128 cu. in. = ?
1 per cent of 128 cu in. = 1.28 cu. in.
27 per cent of 128 cu. in. = 27x1.28 cu. in.
27x1.28 cu. in. = 34.56 cu. in.
∴ 27 per cent of 128 cu. in. = 34.56 cu. in.

Teach the pupil to see the following analysis *in* the form above. Teach the analysis *orally*.

I am required to find 27 per cent of 128 cu. in.: 1 per cent of 128 cu. in. is 1.28 cu. in.; 27 per cent of 128 cu. in. is 27 times 1.28 cu. in.; 27 times 1.28 cu. in. is 34.56 cu. in. Therefore, 27 per cent of 128 cu. in. is 34.56 cu. in.

Give many problems in compound numbers. Spend several days on this work, and give apperception a chance to fulfill its divine mission before taking up another case.

PLAN IV.

I. *Aim:* To find $\frac{2}{3}$ per cent of the length of this window stick.

II. *Method:* The pupils have used this stick in measuring walks, streets, fences, etc. The length of the stick is 6 ft. 8 in. $\frac{2}{3}$ per cent means $\frac{2}{3}$ of 1 per cent. What part of the length of this stick are we to find? "$\frac{2}{3}$ of 1 per cent of the length of the stick." What is the first thing you will do?. "Find 1 per cent of the length of the stick." How will you find this? "Reduce the length to inches, and find $\frac{1}{100}$ of this number of inches." "One per cent of the length of the stick is .8 in." We are to find what? "$\frac{2}{3}$ of 1 per cent of length of the stick."

Solve this and then take a longer distance, as the length of the school-room, and proceed in a similiar way.

—9

Give many oral problems, seven or eight minutes each day. Pupils should be able to handle fractions readily. Problems given by the teacher have a freshness and flavor not found in the book.

PLAN V. CASE III.

I. *Aim:* To find the width of a street 13 per cent of whose width is 7 ft. 9.6 in.

II. *Method:* Pupils repeat the aim. What fact is stated? "13 per cent of the width of the street is 7 ft. 9.6 in." What are you required to find? "The width of the street." Place the fact on the board. The width of the street may be thought of as made up of how many equal parts? "One hundred." Do you know the width of the street? "No." What do you know about the width of the street? "13 hundredths of the width of the street is 7 ft. 9.6 in." How many *hundredths* of the width of the street are you required to find? "One hundred-*hundredths*." How will you proceed? "Find one one-hundredth of the width of the street and multiply this by 100." Put the work on the board in the following form:

7 ft. 9.6 in. is 13 per cent of how wide a street?

13 per cent of the width of the street is 7 ft. 9.6 in., or 93.6 in.

1 per cent of the width of the street is $\frac{1}{13}$ of 93.6 in. which is 7.2 in.

100 per cent of the width of the street is 100 times 7.2 in., which is 720 in. 720 in. is 60 ft.

Therefore, 7 ft. 9.6 in. is 13 per cent of a street 60 ft. wide.

The pupil will be weak for a while in this work. Make many problems for him. Keep him in the realm of sense experience until he comprehends the *principle* involved.

PLAN VI.

I. *Aim:* To think out the following:—$.864 (eighty-six cents four mills) is 20 per cent more than what compound number?

II. *Method:* What fact is stated? "$.864 is 20 per cent more than some number." Is $.864 greater or less than the required number? "Greater." How much greater? "20 per cent greater." The required number is thought of as being made up of one hundred equal parts. The given number is how many hundredths of the required number? "The given number is one hundred twenty-hundredths of the required number." Find one one-hundredth of the required number ($\frac{1}{120}$ of $.864=$.0072). Find one hundred hundredths of the required number (100×$.0072= $.72). $.864 is 20 per cent more than $.72.

PLAN VII.

I. *Aim:* To think out the following: $72. is 20 per cent less than what number of dollars?

II. *Method:* What fact is stated? "$72. is 20 per cent less than some number." The required number is composed of how many equal parts? "One hundred." Of how many *hundredths?* "One hundred *hundredths.*" The given number is how many hundredths of the required number? "The given number is eighty-hundredths of the required number." Find one one-hundredth of the required number ($\frac{1}{80}$ of $72.=$.90). Find one hundred-hundredths of the required number (100×$.90=$90.)

We have not gathered up the statements, rules, and definitions as they have been given or developed. The only new fact, viz.: any quantity or number is made up of one hundred equal parts, is taught upon the *authority* of the teacher. The fact has been illustrated, but not proved. It stands for a *mode of thought* into which the child must grow. These plans have been written and followed in class with the following aims: 1. To exhibit the application of the formal steps (preparation, presentation, comparison, generalization, and application). 2. To set up for the teacher a clearly defined object of thought. 3. To have a clear, definite, and *realizable* aim for pupils and teacher in *teaching* the thought processes involved. 4. To realize the aim by steps in a logical sequence.

These plans are not stereotyped copies of class work. They are rather sign-boards indicating the way we passed and the method. The "applications of percentage" must be taught from the standpoint of the child's interest or he will not make the *application*.

Natural Science.

The natural science lessons of seventh grade come on alternate days, and are mainly oral discussions, for which the teacher must fully prepare himself. It is not expected, however, that the teacher will do the work and the pupils easily accept the fruits of it. Close attention in the classroom, frequent reproductions, both oral and written, a neat and orderly note-book with an abbreviated record of all the topics treated, certain reference work prepared out of class,—these are some of the necessary duties of pupils.

First Term. Fall.

The heart and organs of circulation. Their relation to other internal organs. The effects of alcohol upon the organs of circulation. The previous study of the internal organs of animals will be serviceable and should be called to mind.

The lungs and breathing of animals. In the main, it is a study of human physiology, but the different modes of breathing in animals should be discussed.

The digestive organs in man and in animals. The practical phases of the subject should be discussed before leaving it; the hygiene of eating and of foods, and the effects of alcohol should be noted.

The nervous system, its relation to other organs and to the whole body.

For the Seventh Grade. 125

Second Term. Winter.

Physical Geography.—The relief forms of the continents, as mountains, table lands, plains, etc.

The ocean currents, trade winds, rains, etc.

The distribution of plant and animal life on the globe. The climatic zones, isothermal lines, etc.

The races of man, their characteristics and distribution. See the relations of these topics to the regular geography.

Third Term. Spring.

Botany and *Zoology.*—The processes of growth, development, and seed-production in the vegetable world, illustrated in two or three types, as the elm tree, corn plant, etc., and by reviews of previous studies.

The leading classes of the vegetable kingdom.

The processes of growth and development in animal life. Life history of the horse, spider, etc. Reviews and comparisons. The chief groups or classes of the animal kingdom.

The chief classes of the mineral kingdom.

Use any good text-books in botany, zoology, physical geography, physiology, and geology.

Some of the books to be used are as follows: Guyot's Earth and Man; Parker's How to Teach Geography; Science for All, in four volumes; Gray's Botany; The Hygienic Physiology; Newell's Botany Reader; Comparative Zoology (Orton), and the science primers.

Writing.

The plan for writing outlined by Mr. Cavins will be carried out in the seventh and eighth grades. The system of vertical writing will be taught and practiced in the writing classes and in all written work of the school. The work will be made careful and efficient and children will be excused entirely from the writing drill as soon as their work is satisfactory. They should return to it whenever their usual written work shows serious defects.

Spelling.

Written spelling exercises are conducted daily. Let spelling teachers be clear and definite in their assignments, in pronouncing, and in requiring neat and satisfactory results. Spelling correctors should not allow errors to pass uncorrected. The spelling lessons are taken mainly from the regular lessons in other subjects. Secure an intelligent use of the dictionary.

Music—same as in eighth grade.

Eighth Grade.

The history and literature of this grade will allow the pupils to make a somewhat full acquaintance with some of the great representative characters of American history during this century, and with a number of longer and shorter masterpieces of great authors both in this country and in England. A deep and lasting respect for the ideals of our civilization can be absorbed best from this literature. The biographical element in both the literature and history should be made attractive and instructive. The composition and grammar may be brought into a valuable connection with the literature and both will be helped. Both grammar and arithmetic will be brought to completion so far as it is possible in the grammar school course.

Reading.

First Term. Fall.

Vision of Sir Launfal (Houghton, Mifflin & Co.)
Burke's American Orations (D. C. Heath & Co.)
Selections from Ruskin (Ginn & Co.)

For sight and home reading, The Vicar of Wakefield and Plutarch's Lives. Memorize choice parts from the regular reading, and short poems from Open Sesame, Vol. III, and Heart of Oak, No. V.

Study the Special Method in Reading. Let the teacher make as extensive acquaintance as time permits with all the literature and history recommended for this grade.

Encourage children in home reading and talk with them, recommending suitable books. Get a full amount of expressive oral reading.

Second Term. Winter.

Merchant of Venice. Am. Book Co. Ginn & Co.

Roger de Coverly Papers. Am. Book Co. Houghton, Mifflin & Co.

Emerson's Fortune of the Republic. Houghton, Mifflin & Co.

Webster's Reply to Hayne. Maynard, Merrill & Co.

For sight and home reading, Bacon's Essays and Plutarch's Lives. Compare poems, speeches, and other masterpieces of literature. The purpose of the reading of classics in all these grades is not *criticism*, but appreciation. After children have read and, in a measure, understood a number of the best classics, they may begin to compare and even to form critical judgments. But our aim is chiefly to give children strong impressions from the best writers. Let them first learn to enjoy and appreciate classics.

Third Term. Spring.

Scott's Marmion. Ginn & Co. Houghton, Mifflin & Co. Maynard, Merrill & Co.

Julius Cæsar. Am. Book Co.

Lincoln's Gettysburg Speech, etc. Houghton, Mifflin & Co.

For sight and home reading use Words of Lincoln, Rasselas, and Lady of the Lake.

Study into the biographies of the chief writers, not to gather a few facts, but to understand the life and spirit and character of their efforts and work. The library furnishes good material for references. Connect with the history, geography, and language.

History.

The history for this grade will be the fuller study of a few important topics during the period of the constitution. Not all the important topics can be profitably studied, as some are too difficult.

The work will be partly oral presentation by the teacher, and partly reference-reporting by pupils.

First Term. Fall.

Hamilton's plan and work in launching the financial system of our government.

The rise and influence of political parties up to Jackson's time.

Growth in territory.

Internal improvement.

Causes and results of the war of 1812.

The life of John Quincy Adams.

Webster-Calhoun and nullification.

The wars should not be studied in detail as time is lacking. At most, the principal campaign should be studied.

Second Term. Winter.

History and extension of slavery. The Mexican War. Leading inventions and inventors. Immigration. The life of Daniel Webster. The history of political parties to the Civil War. Study carefully the plan of work outlined in the Special Method in Literature and History for eighth grade.

In all important topics trace out causal relations and see the significance of the more important men and ideas.

Third Term. Spring.

The leading campaigns of the Civil War. Civil Service Reform. Growth of the country since the war. The three departments of our government. The life of Lincoln. The recent history of political parties. The leading questions still unsettled. The books of reference, biography, etc., may be found indicated in the Special Method in Literature and History.

Grammar.

The following outline is a continuation of the plan of work begin in seventh grade by Miss Kate Mavity.

First Term. Fall.

First Month.—*a.* The Noun. Infinitive located. *b.* One composition.

Second Month.—*a.* The Infinitive. *b.* One composition.

Third Month.—*a.* The Pronoun. *b.* One composition.

Second Term. Winter.

First Month.—*a.* The Adjective. *b.* Attributive verb. Participle located. *c.* One composition.

Second Month.—*a.* The Participle. *b.* The Interjection. *c.* The Adverb. *d.* One composition.

Third Month.—*a.* The Verb. *b.* One composition.

Third Term. Spring.

First Month.—*a.* Finish Verb. *b.* The Preposition. *c.* One composition.

Second Month.—*a.* The Conjunction. *b.* Review of Phrases and Clauses. *c.* One composition.

Third Month.—*a.* A classic selection disposed of from the standpoints of Grammar and Composition. *b.* One composition.

The eighth year's work is distinctively a study of the parts of speech. In his seventh year's work the pupil has been introduced to the functions of the sentence and its different parts, and now he is ready to make up the classification and inflection of words. The work to be done is substantially that found in the following outline:

I. THE PARTS OF SPEECH.

1. *Substantive.*

a. Noun.—1 (1). Nature. 2 (1). Classes. *a* (1). On basis of whether an individual or a general idea is expressed.

1 (2). Proper. *a*. (2). Nature. *b* (2). When used. 2 (2). Common. *a* (2). Classes. 1 (3). On basis of whether the object is a natural object or one made out of an attribute. *a* (2). Concrete. 1 (4). Nature. 2 (4). Classes. *a* (4). Unit noun. *b* (4). Multiple noun. *b* (3). Abstract. 1 (4). Nature. 2 (4). Classes. *a* (4). On basis of kind of attribute named. 1 (5). Quality noun. 2 (5). Condition noun. 3 (5). Action noun. *a* (5). Action extinct. *b* (5). Action active—Infinitive. 3 (1). Inflection, or Self-modification. *a* (1). Number. 1 (2). Demand for this inflection. 2 (2). Kinds. *a* 2. Singular. 1 (3). Nature. 2 (3). Spelling. *b* (2). Plural. 1 (3). Nature. 2 (3). Spelling. *b* (1). Gender. 1 (2) Demand for. 2 (2) Kinds. *a* (2). Masculine. *b* (2). Feminine. c (2). Common. *d* (2). Neuter. c (1). Case. 1 (2). Demand for. 2 (2). Kinds. *a* (2). Principal or Nominative. 1 (3). Function. 2 (3). Kinds. *a* (3). Subject. *b* (3). Predicate. c (3). Oppositive to subject or predicate. *b* (2). Subordinate cases. 1 (3). Objective. *a* (3). Nature. *b* (3). Kinds. 1 (4). Object of verb. 2 (4). Object of preposition. 2 (3). Possessive. *a* (3). Nature—Triple function.

b. The infinitive.—Needs separate treatment. 1 (1). Nature. 2 (1). Origin, from pure verb; from attributive verb. 3 (1). Classes on basis of form. *a* (1). The root infinitive, 1 (2). Tense and voice forms. 2 (2). The word "to." *b* (1). The infinite ending in "ing." 1 (2). Tense and voice forms. 4 (1). Uses in the sentence. *a* (1). Natural (by comparison with nouns). *b* (1). Exceptional. 1 (2). Predicate of a clausal phrase. 2 (2). Second part of a double predicate. 5 (1). Modifiers. c. The Pronoun. 1 (1). Nature. 2 (1). Nature. 2 (1). Antecedent. 3 (1). Classes. *a* (1). Personal. 1 (2). Nature. 2 (2). Special inflection. *b* (1). Relative. 1 (2). Double nature. c (1). Interrogative. 1 (2). Nature. *d* (1). Adjective pronoun. *b* (1). Intransitive. 1 (2). Nature. 2 (2). Origin. 2. Attribute. *a*. Adjective. 1 (1). Nature. 2 (1). Classes on basis of kind of attributes objects may have. *a* (1). Quality adjectives. *b* (1). Condition adjectives. *c* (1). Action adjectives. 1 (2). Ordinary action adjectives.

2 (2). *The Participle.* *d* (1). Numeral adjectives. *e* (1). Place adjectives. 3 (1). Inflection. *b.* Attributive verb. 1 (1). Double nature. Comparison with adjective. 2 (1). Kinds. *a* (1). Transitive. 1 (2). Inflection voice.

(c) *Participle.*—1 (1). Nature. 2 (2) Origin, from pure verb; from attributive verb. 3 (1). Uses. (By comparison with adjectives). 4 (1). Modifiers.

(d) *Interjection.*—1 (1) Nature.

(e) *Adverb.*—1 (1). Nature. 2 (1). Classes on basis of kinds of attributes expressed. *a* (1). Time. *b* (1). Place. *c* (1). Cause. *d* (1). Manner. *e* (1). Degree. *f* (1). Negation. *g* (1). Definiteness. 3 (1). Inflection. 3. Relational.

(a) *The verb.*—1 (1). Nature. 2 (1). Classes. *a* (1). The pure verb. 1 (2). Nature. 2 (2). Single function. *b* (1). The attributive verb. 1 (2). Nature. 2 (2). Double function. 3 (1). Inflections. *a* (1). Mode. 1 (2). Defined. 2 (2). Classes. *a* (2). Indicative. *b* (2). Imperative. *c* (2). Subjunctive (?). *d* (2). Potential (?). *b* (1). Tense. 1 (2). Defined. 2 (2). Classes. *a* (2). Present. 1 (3). Meaning. 2 (3). Form. *b* (2). Present perfect. 1 (3). Meaning. 2 (3). Form. *c* (2). Past. 1 (3). Meaning. 2 (3). Form. *d* (2). Past perfect. 1 (3). Meaning. 2 (3). Form. *e* (2). Future. 1 (3). Meaning. 2 (3). Form. *f* (2). Future perfect. 1 (3). Meaning. 2 (3). Form. *c* (1). Number. 1 (2). Defined. 2 (2). Kinds. *a* (2). Singular. *b* (2). Plural. 3 (2). Relation to subject. *d* (1). Person. 1 (2). Defined. 2 (2). Kinds· *a* (2). First. *b* (2). Second. *c* (2). Third. 3 (2). Relation to subject. 3 (1). Principal parts. 4 (1). Derivatives. *a* Of the pure verb. 1 (2). Infinitives. *a* (2). Nature. *b* (2). Forms. *c* (2). Uses. 2 (2). Participles. *a* (2). Nature. *b* (2). Forms. *c* (2). Uses. *b* (1). Of the attributive verb. 1 (2). Infinitives. (Review). 2 (2). Participles. (Review).

b. The Preposition.—1 (1). Nature. 2 (1). Its phrase. 3 (1). Definite meanings of the common prepositions. 4 (1). Special uses of certain prepositions.

c. The Conjunction.—1 (1). Nature. 2 (1). Uses.

A review of phrases and clauses is made after finishing the parts of speech in order to fix the relations of the parts of speech to each other more firmly.

In disposing of the classic selection, which finishes the work of the eighth year, it is thought that almost every point discussed in the two years of composition and grammar will be brought up for review, thus leaving a working knowledge of the subject *fresh* in the pupil's mind.

Natural Science.

The following course of laboratory work is outlined by Mr. J. A. Keith, of the Normal Training School, for the fall and winter terms of eighth grade.

INTRODUCTORY REMARKS.

This outline of laboratory work for the eighth grade requires twenty-seven weeks' time working three periods (forty-five minutes each) a week in the laboratory—and recitations two periods a week. The pupils keep a note book and write up the experiments each day. A great many of the experiments should be performed by the pupils under the direction of the teacher. A clear and definite aim should precede each experiment: an aim with an interest-catching hook to it.

The work on heat has been quite fully outlined: the other subjects are less detailed. Our aim is not to supply the teacher with either knowledge or device, but to suggest a sequence of topics.

The sequence of subjects here presented may be changed to suit the convenience of pupils and teacher. With suitable apparatus the equivalent of this outlined work will be easily done by eighth grade pupils.

REFERENCE BOOKS.

"Nature Study." W. S. Jackman. Henry Holt & Co.

"Home Made Apparatus." J. F. Woodhull. Kellogg & Co.

"Simple Experiments for School Room." J. F. Woodhull. Kellogg & Co.

"First Course in Science." J. F. Woodhull. Henry Holt & Co.

"Physics by Experiment." E. R. Shaw. Effingham, Maynard & Co.

Also note book kept by pupils in physics class in the Illinois State Normal School.

HEAT.

I. *Production.*—1. Produced by friction, percussion, chemical action.

2. Experiments.—(*a*) (1). Rub the hand briskly on the table. (2). Rub two pieces of wood or iron together. (*b*) (1). Hammer a nail vigorously for a few minutes. (2). Put a nail under a moving locomotive wheel. (*c*). To a quantity of water add one-fourth as much sulphuric acid. Notice the action. Feel the tube.

II. *Effects of Heat.*—(*a*). Expansion. (*b*) Combustion—partial, complete.

(*a*) *Expansion, experiments.*—1. Place an alcohol lamp under the rod of a pyrometer. Notice the movement of the index. Explain.

2. Take two pieces of metal, one of which fits an opening in the other. Heat the former. Why can you not put them together now?

3. Take equal-length strips of tin, steel, and brass. Fasten at each end. Heat equally from below. Explain the curvature.

Questions.—What do you conclude regarding the effect of heat on solid metals? Why are rails in railroad track placed so that the ends do not meet? Large brick buildings are often strengthened by having their walls connected by iron rods. Why do mechanics heat these rods when drawing the walls together? Why does a blacksmith heat a wagon tire when he "sets" it? Why do wagon tires often become loose in summer time? [Two reasons]. Constant firing of a target rifle sometimes results in clogging the barrel with bullets. Why? Heat rapidly the inside of a steam pipe. What do you notice?

Have pupils look for other illustrations of the principle involved.

4. Through the cork of a filled bulb tube put a fine glass tube. Nearly fill the tube with water. Heat by holding between the hands. Notice the rise of water in the fine tube. Explain.

5. Put the above apparatus into warm water. Explain results.

6. Put your thumb on the bulb of a thermometer. Explain.

Questions.—What is the effect of heat on liquids? Make a thermometer and determine the zero and boiling points. Teach the use of the thermometer.

7. Fill one bulb tube as in (4) with water. Fill another with alcohol; and a third with kerosene. Put into warm water and note the relative rise in the tubes.

8. Now put the three tubes in cold water and note results.

9. Now put them into a mixture of ice and salt, being careful not to get the mixture above the necks of the tubes. Explain the results.

Questions. Explain the bursting of water mains in midwinter. Which is the heavier, a gallon of water at $8°C$, or one at $48°C$? Why? If an ice-cream freezer be filled with mixture before the freezing begins what will occur as freezing progresses?

9. Invert a partly filled bulb tube in a basin of water. Heat the upper part of the bulb. Notice what happens in the basin and also in the tube. Remove the lamp and note results. Explain.

10. Take an empty thin glass tube, with an *S* tube passing through the cork into the bottle, and put mercury into the lower arm of the *S* tube. Heat the bottle between the hands (or with a lamp) and notice the mercury. Explain.

11. Make a differential thermometer and explain its action.

12. Melt a piece of ice. Evaporate the water.

The effects of heat may be summed up as follows: 1. Change of size: 2, change of temperature: 3. change of state. The *authority* of the teacher must suffice for the melting and vaporization of metals.

Thermometers indicate changes of temperature. The body is not a good test.

13. Prepare a beaker of cold water, one of lukewarm water, and one of warm water. Put the fingers into the cold and warm water. Then put both into the lukewarm water. Explain the sensations.

14. Boil a quantity of water for ten minutes, then measure again. Explain the loss of volume. What becomes of the water when mud dries up? How does water change its form when it evaporates? What is the form before evaporation? Afterward? Is it visible as it passes from the heating pan? Explain. How can vapor be rendered visible? Can you think how the fog is formed? Why do fogs disappear? Explain the Newfoundland fogs. Explain the formation of clouds. When are clouds lowest? Why? Explain the formation of dew. Give the history of a drop of rain.

15. Which is the heavier, a cubic foot of ice or a cubic foot of water? Why? Take a long-necked bulb tube with

a fine tube passing through the cork. Fill the bulb tube with water. Heat slowly, noting rise of water. Cool and pack in ice, keeping the temperature at which the water begins to expand. (Be careful).

Transmission and Phenomena of Heat.—16. Heat one end of a poker, noticing how the heat passes along it. *Conduction.* Hold the hand near different parts of the rod. The hand is warmed by *radiation*. Put some fine, soaked sawdust into a beaker of water and heat slowly. Notice the movements of the particles of sawdust. The heated water rises: the cooler water sinks. Why? Why are not streams as warm as the air in the spring? Why do you "let the bucket sink" in the well when you want a cool drink? How is the heat transmitted when a room is heated by a stove? Steam-pipes and radiators? Furnaces? How is pure air supplied in each case? Illustrate the system of heating by hot-water pipes.

17. Burn paper, soaked with saltpetre, in a chimney, with and without a central strip of tin, both on the table and raised from it. Study ventilation. "Smoke Nuisance."

18. Relative conductive powers of iron, glass, and brass rods. Distribution of heat in a rod heated by conduction. What happens when a warm body is brought into contact with a cooler body? Wrap papers around brass and wooden rods. Hold at equal distances from lamp. Which burns first? Why?

19. Test several thermometers. Put them first into melting ice and then into steam. See if they register correctly. Study the changes preceding and accompanying *boiling*.

20. Study the action of warm water in a closed flask on which cold water is thrown. What about boiling food at high elevations? What about boiling water on high mountains? Under what conditions could you hold your hand in boiling water? Boil water under increased pressure.

21. Study the "still." Distil alcohol from hard cider—apply flame test.

22. Apply equal quantities of heat for equal times to equal weights of different liquids—water, alcohol, kerosene, ammonia. Note results. Teach what is meant by the specific heat of a body. Mix 500 g. of mercury at 8 degrees C. with 500 g. water at 84 degrees C. Find the temperature of the mixture. Which has the greater specific heat? Why?

23. Dip the fingers in ether. Allow them to dry in the air. Dip again. Blow on them. Explain the sensations. Breathe on back of hand. Blow on hand. Explain sensations.

24. Put a few drops of water under a beaker containing a little ether. Blow on the ether with a hand bellows. Explain the result. Visit ice manufactory, or, better still, make some ice.

25. Put as much salt into beakers of water of different temperatures as will readily dissolve. Note the fall in temperatures, and the relative amounts of salt dissolved by waters of different temperatures.

26. Take the temperature of a thermometer under a receiver. Exhaust the air. Explain the fall in temperature.

27. Study the effects of the sun's heat as exhibited by winds—trades, counter trades, constant, monsoon, simoon, variable, a little whirlwind, cyclones, tornadoes, "highs," "lows." Study weather maps.

28. Call to mind that all fuel proceeds or has proceeded from the sun. Compute the power of the sun's rays in evaporating and carrying a recent rainfall.

Combustion.—A term was spent on this work in seventh grade, basing the work on Woodhull's "Simple experiments for the School-Room."

Mechanical Motion from Heat. — Study simple form of engine. Heat overcomes cohesion of water, changing kinetic heat-energy to potential energy (expansive power) of steam. Heat through steam can be changed to motion. Motion can be changed to heat or electricity. Electricity can be changed to heat motion or light.

The following topics are worked out also on a plan similar to the above.

The Mechanical Powers, Gravitation, Hydrostatics, Pneumatics, Light, Sound, Magnetism, Frictional Electricity and Voltaic Electricity.

The science work for SPRING TERM, eighth grade, is as follows:

ELEMENTARY ASTRONOMY.

The teacher may well take the outline and material represented in "Starland" by Sir Robert S. Ball, published by Ginn & Co.

The pupils should keep careful record of the discussions and have frequent tests, oral and written, of their mastery of the work. Other books and charts may be used for reference and illustration.

Arithmetic.

Fall Term.

Review and complete percentage, following the suggestions of Mr. J. A. Keith for seventh grade. Give great variety of familiar application. Oral problems of many varieties should be worked.

Winter and Spring.

Complete Cook and Cropsey's Advanced Arithmetic. Do not limit the work to the text book.

Spelling.

The work is similar to that outlined for seventh grade.

Writing.

The plan of work is the same as in seventh grade.

Music.

The following plan for music in the Grammar school is outlined by Mr. J. A. Keith.

NOTE.—About twenty minutes each day is given to singing. Pupils soon tire of any one *kind* of music work. We indicate below divisions of the work; but the work of any one day includes work from two or more divisions.

I. Songs well known to pupils, to secure interest, confidence, volume, movement, and spirit: America; Star Spangled banner; Marching Thro' Georgia; Battle Hymn of the Republic; Tramp, Tramp, Tramp; The Sleighing Glee; Song of the Grass; Who Was it? Where You See the Angels Stand.

II. The meaning of a few technical terms, as *clef, degree, measure, score, double measure, etc.: quarter-note, etc.; sharp, flat, natural, D. C., Fine, p, pp, f, ff. etc.:* is learned.

III. Reading of simple music in the key of C. A few in other keys. A few well known ones are given below:

Spring is on the Mountain, Sun and Shadow, *Leslie.* Sweet Day, *Pike.* Once More, *Randall.* Spring Song, *Parker.* Onward Marching. *Leslie.* Happy Hearts, *Foudray.* Those Evening Bells, *Beirley.* Song of Spring, *Beirley.* Song of the Grass, *Randall.* The River, *Beirley.* The Coasters, *Pike.* Come Back to Your Home, *Beirley.*

IV. Songs not read by note, but learned by pupils:

Serenade (trio), *Leslie.* Slumber Song, *Leslie.* 'Twas Rum that Spoiled My Boy. Trip Lightly, *Beirley.* Guard Our Nation, *Beirley.* The Moonlight Sail, *Leslie.* Blows the Wind Merrily, *Fargo.* We Come From Fairy Land, *Leslie.* The Old Church Bell, *Beirley.* Beautiful Land, *Pollock.* The Whip-Poor-Will Song, *French.* Beautiful Moonlight, *Beirley.* Vacation Days Are Here, *Johnson.*

Most of these songs are found in "Leslie's Day School Gems," a very cheap, well-bound, and satisfactory book for the grade of pupils.

Consult, also, The Model Music Course, by J. A. Brockhoven and A. J. Gantvoort, published by the John Church Company, Cincinnati, New York, and Chicago. Use the Fourth Reader for grammar school.

Preparatory Class.

This is a class of pupils peculiar to our school. They are seeking suitable preparation for entering the Normal School. The course of study for the term's preparatory work is as follows:

Reading.

Marmion. Ginn & Co. Maynard, Merrill & Co. Houghton, Mifflin & Co.

Seven American Classics. Am. Book Co.

Tales of the White Hills. Houghton Mifflin & Co.

Vision of Sir Launfal. Houghton, Mifflin & Co.

Selections from Ruskin. Ginn & Co.

Tales of Shakespeare. Ginn & Co. Macmillan.

It is not expected that all these will be read, but selections for this class may be made from this list.

These students need to be awakened to the beauties of classic literature. Their imagination should be stimulated. Old habits of monotone and indistinctness should be broken up. Get at the spirit of the reading and drill later for correct rendering.

Geography.

A few of the type studies of North America will be treated completely and then comparisons will be instituted with other similar topics in other continents. Take, *e. g.*, the following types:

The Great Lakes and the St. Lawrence.

The coal mines of Illinois and of the United States.

New York City as a trade-center.

The Mississippi Valley.
The Salt Lake Basin.
The Rocky Mountains.
The Colorado River.
The Cod-fisheries of New Foundland.
The Island of Cuba.
The City of Mexico.

The comparisons may be extended, so far as there is time, to other parts of the world.

Use wall maps. Make the presentations graphic. Assign definite references and not too many or too much at a time. Draw outline maps.

Arithmetic.

Review common and decimal fractions, compound numbers and tests of divisibility.

Give abundance of oral drill. Master the elementary facts and processes of arithmetic. Do thought work. Drill on careful analysis of problems. Illustrate problems with objects and diagrams.

Teacher study Cook's Methods in Written Arithmetic.

Grammar.

In the main follow Miss Mavity's plans as outlined for seventh and eighth grade.

Write a composition once a month.

Dictionary Work.

Take Metcalf and DeGarmo's Dictionary Work, Introduction, Chapter I to Chapter IV, inclusive.

Spelling and Music.

The same plan is followed as in the grammar grades.

A Hand Book.

Of Practical Suggestions for School-room Work.

Discipline.

1. Few and quiet signals are indicative of strength in discipline.
2. Cultivate firmness and decision with gentleness.
3. Do not forget and neglect your own requirements.
4. In cases of difficult management take counsel with the principal, but control the room yourself.
5. Competing with children in smartness is unworthy of a teacher.
6. Be not suspicious and hasty in attributing fault to a child.
7. Assume full responsibility for the class in all respects. Depend on the critic teacher only for outside advice.
8. In exercising discipline use the direct appeal to the principal very seldom. Employ your own tact and invention to meet the emergency. Children respect a teacher who relies on himself.
9. Self-reliance can be strengthened by preparation, will-effort, and experience.
10. Be fair-minded and just.
11. Secure the respect of children by honest dealing.
12. Keeping children after school to learn lessons as a means of punishment is poor policy. But let them do their tasks.
13. Have pupils pass through the halls quietly, promptly, and in line.

14. Use your eyes. See what is going on in the room.

15. Avoid scolding and censuring in the class and before the school. Reprove privately and make it effective.

16. Do not worry over little noises and disturbances if the children are working heartily.

Plan and Preparation.

1. On the back of the plan-book write your name, the term of the year, grade of the class, and subject.

2. In planning a lesson, keep both the children and the subject matter clearly in mind.

3. Each lesson should have a distinct aim, which brings the topics into a natural sequence.

4. The aim should touch the central point of the lesson, approach it from a familiar side, and should be simple and concrete in its statement.

5. A well-planned lesson gives greater freedom for happy inspirations of the moment. Abundant and clear knowledge of the subject is the teacher's best reserve.

6. Have all apparatus—as maps, charts, blocks, pictures, abacus, chalk, board-work—ready before the recitation begins.

7. Mental and physical freshness are so important as to deserve special precaution.

8. Learn to make plans which can be carried out.

9. In case of absence, send written notice in time and send also the plan-book so that the substitute may know just where to take up the lesson.

Assigning Lessons.

1. To assign a lesson well is a difficult and critical thing.

2. Take sufficient time before the end of the period to assign lessons. Five minutes is often insufficient.

3. The aim and preparation, or first step, are often included in the assignment.

4. Be simple and explicit, avoiding all uncertainty.

5. Preparation for the assignment is as important as for the recitation.

6. Create an interest in the new lesson by the manner of assigning it.

7. In using reference books do not work at random. Point out to the children exactly, by volume and page, what they are expected to look for and prepare.

8. Assign short lessons, but insist on thorough mastery.

9. Call to mind previous topics and principles which may be of service in studying the new lesson.

Art of Questioning.

1. It is a difficult art, acquired by preparation, presence of mind, and afterthought.

2. Think twice before asking a question. Do not vary, modify, and correct questions.

3. Make one question go as far as possible. Questions should produce thoughtfulness and reasoning.

4. Questions designed to test knowledge acquired should not be helps to the pupil.

5. The honest questions of children should be respected. But many children abuse their privilege and should be checked.

6. General, indefinite questions are often blind. Most questions should be specific.

7. Do not waste time in guessing, in questions which children cannot answer.

Securing and Holding the Attention.

1. To strengthen the habit of attentiveness in children should be a fundamental aim of the teacher. Teachers are too careless about holding the attention of the whole class.

2. Involuntary attention depends upon interest in the

subject. Voluntary attention depends, first, upon the will of the teacher; secondly, upon the will of the pupil.

3. The position of teacher and pupils should aid attention.

4. Recess and gymnastic exercises between the periods are a direct support to attention.

5. A pure text-book method is unfavorable to attention.

6. Laxity of attention is a striking weakness of our schools. In oral recitations, where no text-book is used, everything depends upon attentiveness. The habit of inattention, cultivated in the class-room, repeats and strengthens itself in the home studies of children.

7. You will not get good work of any kind by simply asking for it, but by insistence.

8. Provide for good variety of work during a recitation.

9. Weak control and weak instruction leave a class in the condition of an unstrung violin. No response can be elicited.

Instruction.

1. The teacher is a guide rather than a lecturer.

2. Few teachers realize what it is to treat subjects *concretely* and *inductively*. Most text-books are abstract rather than concrete, deductive rather than inductive, and teachers must make good these deficiencies. A teacher should be full of resources, devices, and information. Fertility in device, in illustration, in graphic drawing, should be a professional characteristic. From your own resources, add vividness and reality to the contents of the text-book. Study home surroundings and experience as a means of illustration. Have children do the same.

3. Study the general plan and purpose of your text-book.

4. Loud and persistent talking by a teacher is a bad sign. A teacher should be laconic and the master of his

tongue. The more a teacher is habituated to talking, the less the pupils think.

5. Do not explain what some member of the class can explain.

6. Require pupils to reproduce all facts and explanations given by the teacher.

7. On the other hand, a teacher should talk to the best effect when occasion requires. In the oral presentation of a new lesson to a class, the teacher should cultivate a special skill and vividness in narration and description.

8. Strictly oral lessons in natural science, literature, history-stories, and geography, require a very clear and logical *outline of points* for each lesson. It should be put on the board by the teacher during the recitation, and each part should be carefully reproduced by the children. The outline should be copied also into blank books in ink, as the basis of future reviews.

10. In general do not tell the class anything which is not reproduced during the same lesson by the children.

Board Work.

1. There is always a temptation for teachers to be hasty and carless in board work, done before the class. Such work should be a model of neatness. Overcome the spirit of hurry and flurry.

2. Keep the boards free from careless and unnecessary marks. Each teacher should leave the boards in good shape.

3. Copying lessons from the board should be avoided as much as possible.

4. Children should be kept strictly independent of one another in board work.

5. Let the board work of pupils be careful and thoughtful. Check the habit of erasing and re-writing.

6. One teacher should not monopolize board room with written work at the expense of others.

Personal Manner.

1. Acquire self-control and confidence.
2. A sincere and hearty manner is very desirable.
3. Social tact is all important to a teacher.
4. Confidence in the pupils and sympathy for them encourage like feelings in them.
5. The easy and unostentatious habits of a gentleman are not acquired in a moment, but by close observation, thoughtfulness and goodness of heart.
6. Awkward positions and motions should be studiously avoided.
7. Some of the best people have the most obnoxious faults and never find them out. Neatness of dress, clean teeth, and well-kept hands and finger-nails have become standard requirements.
8. Do not get too close to the children in recitation work. They will speak, read, etc., with more force and independence at a little distance from the teacher. Do not fondle older pupils.

Position and Manners of Children.

1. Let them sit and stand squarely, and talk clearly and forcibly.
2. The selfish prominence of some children in recitation should be checked, while the timid ones should be encouraged.
3. Children should be required to show a kindly and respectful manner to schoolmates as well as to teachers. The behavior of children should be as quiet and courteous in school as when visiting or receiving friends at home.
4. The room, desks, and floor should be kept as neat and orderly as the best room at home. Be very careful to avoid ink stains on desks and floors.
5. See that children's names are well written in all their books. Prevent scribbling in their books.

6. Scraps of paper should be kept from the floor and desks.

7. Be careful about excusing children from the room. Keep a record and report such cases to the room-teacher.

8. Do not waste paper or any materials furnished by the school.

9. Let children keep their hands clean and their person neat.

☐ 10. Written papers, handed in to a teacher, should be clean, with well-cut edges, and adequate in size for good work.

Observing Others' Teaching.

1. Be able to discover quickly the strong and the weak points in others' teaching. Give reasons.

2. Find out beforehand the teacher's plan for the lesson.

3. Do not rely chiefly upon memory for the criticism of a lesson.

4. Our faults and merits are often seen magnified in the teaching of others. The suggestions thus derived may be very helpful.

5. Make your criticisms specific, and base them upon established principles. Be able to point out clearly the remedy.

6. Study the chapter on instruction.

7. Do not write up a great quantity of details, but give definite and pointed criticism.

8. Do not forget the recitation and its plan in the criticism of discipline.

Self-Criticism.

1. Bad habits or tendencies should be discovered and corrected at the beginning of experience in teaching.

2. Severe and effective self-criticism in teaching is wisdom.

3. Do not be offended easily at criticisms.

4. Do not think too much about yourself while teaching,

but allow the interest in the lesson to carry you along vigorously.

5. Review your lessons thoughtfully and consider where you might have improved the plan or its execution.

6. Be reasonable in acknowledging your mistakes to children.

Observation of Children.

1. Some children need to be carefully studied by the teacher, because of their peculiar disposition.

2. A knowledge of the home surroundings and habits of a child may help the teacher to appreciate and sympathize with him.

3. Personal and kindly conversation with a child when school is not in session will often help both teacher and pupil.

4. The practice of making a close study of at least one child each term will give the teacher much suggestion and tact in treating other children.

5. Be careful to notice whether some children are poor of hearing, near-sighted, or weak physically in any way. Adapt conditions to such needs.

6. Observe children on the play-ground, on excursions, etc., where they express their disposition and their individuality more freely.

Reporting Children.

1. The study hour is the time when the room-teacher can attend to backward and deficient pupils, as well as assist all children reasonably in their allotted studies.

2. Each teacher of a class should daily interview those children who are negligent in their work or who, for any culpable reason, neglect the full performance of their duties.

The class-teacher should also report daily to the room-teacher such special pupils as for neglect of their work need special attention during the study hours.

By looking at the list of names filed on his desk daily,

the room-teacher may aid greatly in keeping each child up to the requirements.

Promotions.

1. Pupils in a class, who are manifestly graded too high or too low for the class in which they recite. should be promptly reported to the critic teacher.

2. Occasional promotions or reductions, if wisely made, have an excellent tonic effect.

3. A bright child sometimes does poor work in a class because the work is too easy for him. Promote him and lay heavier burdens upon him.

Consult with parents about promotions and be considerate of all the circumstances.

Teachers' Responsibility for Suggestions in the Hand Book.

1. Pupil teachers should make constant use of the Hand Book and keep its injunctions and suggestions in mind. This is true especially at the beginning of the term.

2. The references to Special Methods in Geography, Reading, Literature and History, and Natural Science should be read and applied in class-room work.

3. Let practicing teachers apply to the critic teachers for necessary desk-books, paper, and other materials. Report pupils promptly who are not supplied with text-books.

General Spirit in a Class or School Room.

1. Let children learn to help each other in a kindly spirit.

2. Incidents in the room give opportunity to apply many lessons learned from books.

Records and Standing of Children.

1. Each teacher may keep in a private note book such record of the class work as seems helpful.

2. Once a week let each teacher record in the class

record (kept at the room-teacher's desk), an estimate of each pupil's work. Let these reports be made with care and promptness. (This is for intermediate and grammar grades.)

3. At the end of each month a card report is sent by the room-teacher to the parents for each child.

Relation to Critic Teachers, Plan Books, etc.

1. After a visit from the critic teacher, the practicing teacher should take the earliest opportunity to visit the critic teacher and receive the criticisms.

2. Each practicing teacher must hold himself responsible for reaching his classes on time, both in the Normal School and in the Training School.

3. Each teacher of a class is expected to leave his or her plan-book on the desk of the critic teacher each Monday morning, before 8:30, with the plans of lessons made out a week ahead.

Notes on Critique-Lessons.

1. The practicing teachers are divided into three groups, the Primary, Intermediate, and Grammar.

2. Once a week, at an appointed time, each of these groups attends a critique-lesson, taking careful notes, which are preserved in the plan-books.

3. Each teacher is required to attend one regular critique-lesson a week, and write up the notes upon it.

4. On Monday afternoon, from 3 to 4 o'clock, the last regular critique-lesson is discussed, under the direction of the critic teacher of that group.

5. The term *critique-lesson* is simply a brief term to express an illustrative lesson presented to a group of teachers for close observation and criticism.

6. The criticisms and final conclusions relative to each critique-lesson should be entered briefly but pointedly in the plan-book, in a separate place.

PRICE LIST OF
HERBARTIAN PUBLICATIONS.

DISCUSSION OF PRINCIPLES.

McMurry's General Method is a book of 224 pages which gives a clear and interesting statement of the principles of teaching. It is being used in teachers' clubs that are formed in many cities and towns. Price, 75 cents, postpaid.

The Method of the Recitation. (*In Press.*) This volume is a sequel to the General Method, and is the combined work of Dr. Frank McMurry and Dr. Chas. A. McMurry in applying the principles of General Method to class-room instruction in the different studies. Price, post-paid, $1.

APPLICATION OF PRINCIPLES TO SPECIAL STUDIES.

McMurry's Books on Special Method.

Literature and History in Primary Grades................................ 25c
Geography Through the Fourth Grade (225 pp.).................... 40c
Reading in Primary and Grammar Grades................................ 30c
Science in Lower Grades. (*In Press.*)...................................... 30c

All bound in flexible cloth covers.

BOOKS OF MATERIAL TO BE USED BY THE PUPILS.

Classic Stories for the Little Ones, by Lida B. McMurry, is a beautifully illustrated volume of Fairy Tales and Folk-lore written for children in the first and second grades. The teachers' edition contains full instructions and suggestions on the purpose and method of teaching each story. No such book has ever before been published. It is now ready. Price (postpaid), teachers' ed., 40c; child's ed., 35c.

Robinson Crusoe for Boys and Girls, by Lida B. McMurry and Mary Hall Husted, is another book of material to be used by the pupil in second and third grade, in the study of literature and history. It is a transition book from fairy tales to real history, and the Pioneer History Stories are intended to follow it. Teachers' and mothers' ed. sent (postpaid), for 40c; child's ed. sent (postpaid), for 35c.

The Tales of Troy, by Dr. Chas. DeGarmo, is a series of stories for boys and girls, that is intended to assist in the study of literature and history in the grammar grades. The entire history of the siege and capture of ancient Troy, as told by Homer and Virgil, is given in these stories. Price, cloth, postpaid, 40c.

McMurry's Pioneer History Stories is a book of material for the use of the pupils in fourth and fifth grades. It is to accompany the study of the geography of the Mississippi Valley, and Rocky Mountain region. It is a companion to Methods in Geography. Price, 50c, postpaid.

McMurry's Pioneer Explorers on Land and Sea. (*In Press.*) Stories of early explorers and settlers along the Atlantic sea-board, and of early navigators—Columbus and Magellan. These stories run parallel with the geography of the fifth grade, and are more directly introductory to the early history of our country. Price, 50c, postpaid.

Course of Study for the Eight Grades. Price, 40c.

Dr. Harris' Report on Correlation of Studies, with annotations by George P. Brown. 20c.

Address

PUBLIC-SCHOOL PUBLISHING CO.,

www.ingramcontent.com/pod-product-compliance
Lightning Source LLC
Chambersburg PA
CBHW030319170426
43202CB00009B/1069